E.R. Braithwaite

TO SIR, WITH LOVE

adapted for the stage by
Ayub Khan-Din

NICK HERN BOOKS

London
www.nickhernbooks.co.uk

A Nick Hern Book

This stage adaptation of *To Sir, With Love* first published in Great Britain in 2013 as a paperback original by Nick Hern Books Limited, The Glasshouse, 49a Goldhawk Road, London W12 8QP

Reprinted 2017

To Sir, With Love copyright © 1959 E.R. Braithwaite
First published in Great Britain by The Bodley Head, 1959
Stage adaptation of *To Sir, With Love* copyright © 2013 Ayub Khan-Din

Ayub Khan-Din has asserted his right to be identified as the author of this adaptation

Cover image: Feast Creative
Cover design: Ned Hoste, 2H

Typeset by Nick Hern Books, London
Printed and bound in Great Britain by Mimeo Ltd, Huntingdon, Cambridgeshire
PE29 6XX

A CIP catalogue record for this book is available from the British Library

ISBN 978 1 84842 370 1

Woodland CARBON
www.woodlandcarbon.co.uk
NICK HERN BOOKS
Printed on Carbon Captured paper

E.R. BRAITHWAITE

E.R. Braithwaite was born in Guyana in 1912. He served as a fighter pilot with the RAF during World War II and then studied at Caius College, University of Cambridge, gaining a BA and then an MSc in Physics.

He worked as a schoolteacher in the East End of London from 1951 to 1958, before becoming a welfare consultant with London County Council. In 1960, he was appointed secretary to the World Veterans Federation in Paris, and then education consultant to UNESCO in Paris in 1962. He served as permanent representative of Guyana to UN in New York from 1967 to 1969, followed by three years as Guyana's ambassador to Venezuela. He returned to teaching in 1973 when he was appointed professor of English at New York University, and then became writer-in-residence at Florida State University from 1976 to 1977. After many years writing and lecturing, he became writer-in-residence at Howard University, Washington, DC, from 1998 to 2004.

To Sir, With Love was his first book, written in 1959. Later publications include: *Paid Servant, A Kind of Homecoming, Choice of Straws, Reluctant Neighbours, Honorary White* and *Billingsly: the Bear With the Crinkled Ear*.

AYUB KHAN-DIN

Ayub Khan-Din's play *East is East* (1997) was staged at the Royal Court Theatre and adapted into a feature film. The play and film have won a Writer's Guild Award for Best New Writer and a British Academy Award. Other plays include *Last Dance at Dum Dum* (1999), *Notes on Falling Leaves* (2004) and *Rafta, Rafta...* (2007), which won a Laurence Olivier Award for Best New Comedy. A film adaptation, *All in Good Time,* was released in 2012, a year after his sequel to *East is East,* named *West is West.* His most recent plays have been *All the Way Home,* directed by Mark Babych at the Lowry Theatre in Salford, and musical comedy *Bunty Berman Presents,* produced on Broadway by The New Group.

This adaptation of *To Sir, With Love* was first performed at
Royal & Derngate, Northampton (James Dacre, Artistic Director;
Martin Sutherland, Chief Executive), on 10 September 2013
(previews from 7 September), with the following cast:

DENHAM	Mykola Allen
MONICA	Harriet Ballard
GILLIAN	Peta Cornish
SEALES	Kerron Darby
RICKY	Ansu Kabia
FLORIAN	Matthew Kelly
WESTON	Paul Kemp
PAMELA	Heather Nicol
CLINTY	Nicola Reynolds
COMMUNITY	Ben Ayers, Alana Castle, Sasha
ENSEMBLE	Farmer, George Attwell Gerhards,
	Christian Needle, Cameron Percival,
	Poppy Roberts, Isobel Scanlon

Director	Mark Babych
Designer	Mike Britton
Lighting Designer	Johanna Town
Sound Designer	Ivan Stott
Choreographer	
& Movement Director	Nick Winston
Fight Director	Philip d'Orléans
Associate Director	
& Associate Producer	Neale Birch
Casting Director	Camilla Evans
Deputy Stage Manager	Jo Phipps

Scenery, set painting, properties, costuming, wigs and make-up
by Royal & Derngate workshops and facilitated in-house by
stage-management and technical teams.

The production subsequently toured to New Theatre, Cardiff; Everyman Theatre, Cheltenham; Theatre Royal, Nottingham; Wolverhampton Grand Theatre; King's Theatre, Edinburgh; Alhambra Theatre, Bradford; Darlington Civic Theatre; Oxford Playhouse; Orchard Theatre, Dartford.

To Sir, With Love was commissioned by Mark Goucher, Jenny King and Matthew Gale for The Touring Consortium Theatre Company, and produced by Jenny King and Royal & Derngate, Northampton.

For Miss Snowdon,
Ordsall Board School, Salford 1966/1970

Who taught me to read and showed me
the world beyond my own.

Characters

MR LEON FLORIAN, *fifty-five, headmaster*
VIVIENNE CLINTRIDGE 'CLINTY', *thirty-five, teacher*
RICARDO BRAITHWAITE 'RICK', *thirty-one, teacher*
GILLIAN BLANCHARD, *twenty-one, teacher*
HUMPHREY WESTON, *thirty-nine, teacher*

THE SENIOR CLASS
PAMELA DARE, *fourteen*
MONICA PAGE, *fourteen*
DENHAM, *fourteen*
SEALES, *fourteen, mixed-race English-Nigerian*
ESTHER JOSEPH, *fourteen*
ARCHIE, *fourteen*
EDWARD EDWARDS, *fourteen*
JANE PURCELL, *fourteen*
FERNMAN
ROSE
NORA
YOUTH GROUP KIDS

This text went to press before the end of rehearsals and so may differ slightly from the play as performed.

ACT ONE

London 1948

Scene One

The staffroom of a large Victorian school in the East End of London, 1948. The room is untidy, filled with books, odd bits of sports equipment, coats and bags. There is a torn poster from the 1948 Olympics. The mantelpiece is loaded with cups. A door to the side leads off to a toilet. In the centre of the room, a large table covered with newspapers and magazines. Various armchairs are placed around in no particular order. We can hear the sounds of children from the playground. A small coffee table has been turned over. VIVIENNE CLINTRIDGE *is on her hands and knees picking up some broken crockery.* GILLIAN BLANCHARD *is mopping the floor.* HUMPHREY WESTON *is sat in an armchair, legs hooked over the arm; watching the women clean, he is lighting a pipe.*

Enter MR LEON FLORIAN. *In the background we can hear children shouting an un-cherubic version of 'We are the Ovaltineys'.*

MR FLORIAN. I've just been informed. Was it ugly?

WESTON. Let's say I don't think we'll be seeing our esteemed colleague amongst these hallowed halls of enlightenment again.

MR FLORIAN. Is he still around? Maybe I could talk to him.

CLINTY. It's gone quite beyond that, I'm afraid.

GILLIAN. And he seemed such a quiet sort of chap.

WESTON. He'll have reached divisional office by now. Demanding a more salubrious relocation. Listen to those obnoxious little toads!

We can hear the senior class shouting 'The Ovaltineys' theme.

WESTON. Bloody Eviltineys more like!

CLINTY. He seemed perfectly fine this morning. Did you upset him, Weston?

WESTON. Me? I'm shocked you should even think that way, Clinty. I barely said a word to the man. He walked in. Sat in that chair and the next thing I know, he went completely doolally tap. Ranting and raving like a madman.

GILLIAN. I offered him a coffee.

WESTON. That'd be it then. It's your fault. He drinks tea. 'White, weak, half-sugared.' Very particular was our Mr Hackman. If you get my drift.

MR FLORIAN. Really, Mr Weston –

WESTON. Let's face it, Headmaster. The man, just wasn't man enough to deal with that class. Christ! The Waffen SS would be hard pushed!

MR FLORIAN. Mr Weston, I know it's your free period after break but could you –

WESTON. No, I could not. It's bad enough dealing with my own little monsters without taking on board their delinquent elder siblings.

CLINTY. That's the Dunkirk spirit, Weston.

WESTON. I wouldn't touch them with a six-foot pole or a Yugoslav for that matter.

CLINTY. I'll bring them over into mine. They won't mess with me.

MR FLORIAN. Thank you so much, Miss Clintridge. It'll just be for the first period, then I'll take over for the rest of the day. I'd take them myself now, only I've a meeting with the education office.

WESTON. More bad news on the horizon?

MR FLORIAN. I certainly hope not, Mr Weston. But they do like to keep abreast of the way we work here.

WESTON. Not going to be too happy with the Hackman episode then, are they?

MR FLORIAN. It's nothing that doesn't happen at any other school in the country.

GILLIAN *heads off to the toilet through the door by the fireplace.*

WESTON. Only it happens here with such alarming regularity.

CLINTY. Do get to your point, Weston.

WESTON. I'm merely saying that if there were more discipline in the classroom, we'd have firmer control over the children, which in turn would put a halt to the hysterical happenings of this morning repeating themselves.

CLINTY. Spare the rod, spoil the child?

WESTON. Well, at least we'd all know exactly where we stood. Them as well as us. It's just as important for them to understand the parameters.

MR FLORIAN. You know my thoughts on corporal punishment, Mr Weston.

WESTON. Yes, Headmaster. But when it comes to running a classroom there has to be some rules.

MR FLORIAN (*good-naturedly*). Ahh, rules. But to what purpose, Mr Weston. To what end? Who gains more from rules you or the children? To rule, Mr Weston. You want to rule in your classroom? Do you want to be king of all you survey?

WESTON. No, Headmaster, I'm merely pointing out that –

MR FLORIAN. We must be careful of rules; rules have a way of ruling. These children are surrounded by rules, their whole –

There is a knock on the door.

Enter! Their whole lives, from the –

The door opens and standing there is RICARDO BRAITHWAITE, *a black, thirty-one-year-old West Indian. He's dressed smartly in his demob suit. Everyone turns and stares at him.*

Good heavens, Mr Braithwaite. I'd quite forgotten about you in all the excitement. Come in, come in, my dear fellow.

Everyone, this is Mr Braithwaite. He's come to take a look at us – the school that is – with the prospect of joining our ranks if we pass muster.

All smile encouragingly to him. All except WESTON.

WESTON. Another sheep to the slaughter. Or should that be a black sheep?

No one says anything. The comment hangs in the air until the silence is broken by the school bell. Everyone starts to head out of the door.

MR FLORIAN. Always the way, I'm afraid, Braithwaite. Little matter! You can meet them all properly at lunch. Meanwhile, I too must abandon you. But do have a wander about the place. I'll join you just as soon as I can, then maybe we can have a chat about what you think of us. If indeed we are your cup of tea – no pressure. No pressure at all. Though I might add we suddenly find ourselves bereft of another member of staff – again. Rather careless I know, but these things happen. But as I said, no pressure. Tea in the urn! Cheerio!

MR FLORIAN *heads out of the door. Leaving* RICK *alone in the staffroom. He looks about the room. He walks over to the window and looks out. He goes over to the table and flicks a few pages of a paper. He just stands there not knowing what to do with himself. We hear a toilet flush.* GILLIAN *comes in and jumps when she sees* RICK.

GILLIAN. Arrrh!… I'm sorry you startled me –

RICK *smiles and proffers his hand.*

RICK. Ricardo Braithwaite.

She takes it and shakes it rather too enthusiastically.

GILLIAN. Gillian, I'm Gillian Blanchard. Lovely to meet you.

RICK *has to pull his hand away gently.*

Sorry…

Pause. They look at each other. He smiles.

RICK. I'm here to look at the school.

GILLIAN. Ah – you're from the divisional office, come to check up on us.

RICK *looks confused.*

RICK. No, I might be joining the staff.

GILLIAN. Oh, I see – Gosh, that was quick.

RICK. What was?

GILLIAN. You replacing our Mr Hackman. He's only been gone an hour.

RICK. I'm not here to replace anyone.

GILLIAN. Oh, hell – Of course you're not. That would be quick – and far too efficient. Maybe I should just come back in again.

She smiles.

Would you like a cup of tea?

RICK. Yes. Please.

GILLIAN *proceeds to pour tea from a tea urn into a cup.*

GILLIAN. Milk and sugar?

RICK. One sugar. No milk.

GILLIAN. It might be a bit stewed. There are some biscuits in that Oxo tin over there, if you fancy.

He walks over to the tin.

It's usually well stocked from what the girls in domestic science knock out. I'm afraid the taste varies from batch to batch and year to year – In fact, don't have a biscuit.

RICK. No?

GILLIAN. I think they were made by first years and they haven't quite grasped the concept of hygiene.

She passes him the tea.

Do sit down.

RICK. What happened?

GILLIAN. Sorry?

RICK. To your, Mr Hackman?

GILLIAN. Oh, unable to handle the kids – so they say or rather Weston says. You may have seen him earlier – Weston that is – he's maths – with the beard.

    RICK *smiles*.

RICK. Are the children difficult to manage?

GILLIAN. Hard to say really, I've only been here a couple of weeks myself. So I'm not the right person to ask. They seem okay.

    Beat.

    It is different; this school. You do know that? About the school – the headmaster?

RICK. I don't know anything.

GILLIAN. There's no corporal punishment for starters. Any form of punishment for that matter, and the children are encouraged to speak up for themselves.

RICK. Really?

GILLIAN. They write their own reports – on us and the school… Student councils, that sort of thing.

RICK. That sounds interesting.

GILLIAN. Unfortunately they're not always particularly choosy about what they say and the manner in which they say it. They can be rather alarming reads at times.

RICK. They unnerve you?

GILLIAN. No, not really. They're just so frightfully grown-up, some of them. The girls have a way of looking at me, sort of pityingly, as if they're so much older and wiser than I am. I think they're more interested in my clothes and private life than anything I try to teach them. They're obsessed with knowing if I have a boyfriend or not.

RICK. Maybe it's your youth, they're playing on your inexperience.

GILLIAN. You mean they can smell fresh meat.

RICK. I wouldn't say that.

GILLIAN. I would.

Enter CLINTY.

CLINTY. Hello again, just got to grab a couple of things.

She picks up a piece of newspaper, goes over to a cupboard and takes out a packet of Dr White's sanitary towels. She proceeds to wrap them up in the newspaper.

Sorry, Gillian, could I steal you away to fix a bath, for the Murphy girl. Kids are complaining of the smell again. Won't sit near her.

RICK. What's the matter with the child? Enuretic?

CLINTY *looks at him.*

CLINTY. Good God no! She's been wearing the same sanitary towel for days.

RICK. Oh, I...

RICK *is lost for words.* GILLIAN *inadvertently raises her hand to her mouth.*

CLINTY. Child stinks to high heaven. Fourteen years old and as helpless as an infant. Some mothers ought to be shot.

Beat.

(*Laughing.*) You should see the look on your faces! This is teaching, my dears. Front-line stuff. You're well and truly in the trenches here.

Scene Two

Same day. Staffroom. MR FLORIAN *leans over the staff table looking at a paper.* RICK *comes in.*

MR FLORIAN. Ah, there you are, Braithwaite. Had a good look about the place?

RICK. Yes.

MR FLORIAN. Do you know London at all?

RICK. I took some leave here during the war, so I know it as a tourist. And of course from what I've gleaned from Chaucer and Pepys.

MR FLORIAN. Yeeeeees... Well, I think Samuel Pepys would have a good deal more to add to his diaries, if he'd been here during the blackout! Now that would be a good read!

RICK. Indeed, sir.

MR FLORIAN. Now, before we take the next step, I want to outline how we do things here. You may agree or disagree. Either way I expect you to be honest and say so. That's part of my position on teaching. Honesty – clear and simple. If we can't be honest amongst ourselves, how on earth can we be honest with the children.

RICK. Yes, sir.

MR FLORIAN. Most of our children, have been classified as difficult. Their experiences in their junior schools, positive or negative, they carry over to us. That's five years of rules and regulations. Never having to think for themselves, learning everything by rote and God forbid, if a child can't keep up...

MR FLORIAN *takes* RICK*'s arm and walks him over to the window.*

Look at this place, Mr Braithwaite.

RICK *walks over to him.*

All over this country, young minds are being shaped by similar stinking environments. Poverty, unemployment. We can't blame the war, things were just as bad before. How can we expect children who grow up in these conditions, to take seriously, anything we have to teach them. What do they care about arithmetic, when their main concern is whether they'll go home to a hot meal – any meal for that matter. Us threatening punishment means nothing to them. It's just another endurance in a life full of daily endurances.

He turns to RICK.

What I'm trying to do here, is to create an atmosphere, where young people can feel safe, wanted and secure. Free to work, play and express themselves. For a few hours of their day, they will be guided by adults who will listen to them, who care about their opinions, who try to understand without condemnation. Well, there it is. I can offer you no blueprint for teaching, it wouldn't work, especially here. You're on your own. The rest of the staff, myself included, will always be ready to help and advise if need be.

RICK. I don't know what the department has told you about me, Headmaster. But I think it only right that you should know, that I've had no experience of teaching or any form of training.

MR FLORIAN. Oh, I know. I've seen your file.

RICK. Then you'll know that teaching was not my first choice of profession.

MR FLORIAN. No; I should have thought that a man with your outstanding qualifications would have chosen something quite different for himself. Electronics, wasn't it?

RICK. Yes.

MR FLORIAN. Well, then it's our good fortune that you have decided to teach for now.

RICK. I'm reading a lot of books on teaching and teaching methods –

MR FLORIAN. Oh, my dear fellow, you don't want to do that.

RICK. No?

MR FLORIAN. Good heavens, no, I'd rather have you and all that you've seen and done with your life, than some wet-behind-the-ears novice with umpteen teaching certificates. Now then, what is it to be? 'Is Barkis willing?'

RICK. Have you had any thought as to what class I'd be teaching?

MR FLORIAN *thinks for a moment.*

MR FLORIAN. You'll have charge of the top class.

RICK. Your Mr Hackman's class?

MR FLORIAN. Yes, our Mr Hackman. Unfortunately Mr Hackman, though a perfectly adequate teacher, was completely unsuitable for this kind of work.

RICK. Really?

MR FLORIAN. Look, I'm not offering you the booby prize, Mr Braithwaite. They're an important class, they need the influence of a good teacher, particularly as they'll be leaving us shortly. I think you're the man for the job.

Beat.

RICK. Then you can tell Peggotty, that 'Barkis is willing'.

MR FLORIAN. Good man!

The school bell sounds.

RICK. When would you like me to start?

We hear the sounds of excited children and doors slamming. MR FLORIAN *heads out as* CLINTY *comes in followed by* GILLIAN *and* WESTON.

MR FLORIAN. I'm pleased to announce, Mr Braithwaite, is going to be joining the staff.

CLINTY. Good for you.

MR FLORIAN. I hope you'll all make him very welcome.

MR FLORIAN *heads out.*

Back in a minute.

GILLIAN. Which class have you got?

RICK. Hackman's.

WESTON. May the Lord God, have mercy on your poor soul.

He goes over to the fireplace and takes out his pipe.

I suppose the old man gave you all the old blather about these poor deprived angels?

CLINTY. Ignore him.

She holds out her hand.

I'm Vivienne Clintridge, domestic science, art and drama. Welcome aboard. It's not too bad here. They might bark but they don't bite. That's pretty good odds in my book. And regardless of anything else you might hear – Weston! – The old man knows exactly what he's doing.

WESTON. You'll be sharing PE duties with me, he did tell you that? There's no negotiation.

RICK. Well –

WESTON. – No, there's no crying off, I saw your lot doing track and field in the Olympics. So I know you can run and chuck things about!

RICK. I was about to say, I'll look forward to it.

Beat.

WESTON. Oh, will you now.

CLINTY. How wonderful to have a new man about the place.

WESTON *gives her a dismissive look and starts to light his pipe.*

WESTON. Careful, Clinty, your psyche is showing.

CLINTY. Always does when I'm close to a real man, Weston. Been in the country long?

GILLIAN. Clinty!

CLINTY. Only asking. Nothing wrong in a bit of background information, is there, Braithwaite?

RICK. Certainly not. I've been here since '39. I came to enlist.

CLINTY. Good for you. What service?

RICK. RAF. I flew fighters.

CLINTY. My brother was RAF Bombers... Didn't make it unfortunately.

RICK. I'm sorry.

CLINTY. Thank you.

WESTON. I didn't know we were that hard up, that we had people of your persuasion in the RAF. Canteen staff, was it?

RICK. I flew Spitfires actually... When I wasn't too busy polishing the mess silver.

GILLIAN. We had men from all over the Empire fighting and dying for us, Mr Weston. If you've forgotten just how big and diverse the Empire is, I suggest you sit in on one of my classes.

WESTON. Getting smaller by the minute, isn't it? I should think by lunchtime we'd have lost most of the Far East.

CLINTY. You didn't serve did you, Weston?

WESTON. Unfortunately, I have flat feet.

CLINTY. And a flat personality to match!

> WESTON *heads out of the room.*

> Glad you joined us, Braithwaite. Look, don't mind Weston, there's one in every staffroom and unfortunately he's ours.

> MR FLORIAN *pops his head around the door.*

MR FLORIAN. Come along, Braithwaite, we'll go and have some lunch.

> *The lights fade and we hear King Perry singing 'Going to California'.*

Scene Three

Lights up in the school gym. There are a number of BOYS *and* GIRLS *aged fourteen to fifteen. They are jiving to King Perry singing 'Going to California'. Others stand around watching. The dancers are extremely proficient as they exercise energetic moves.* RICK *and* MR FLORIAN *walk into the gym.*

MR FLORIAN. What do you think?

RICK. Erm…

MR FLORIAN. Their idea. Voted for by the student council. They're good, aren't they? Oh, well done, Pamela!

RICK. I'm impressed.

MR FLORIAN. Do you dance?

RICK. Are you asking?

MR FLORIAN *laughs.*

MR FLORIAN. Good heavens, no! I couldn't possibly expect you to keep up with me. Besides, I always lead.

RICK. You said they voted for this?

MR FLORIAN. Yes. Student council. Head boy and girl and their two deputies, all voted in by the other students. They're in on all decision-making here.

RICK. How far are we supposed to take this… student council?

MR FLORIAN. Sorry, not with you?

RICK. Well, what exactly are they allowed to vote for?

MR FLORIAN. Ah, yes. Good point.

RICK *waits for an answer but* MR FLORIAN *has turned back to watch the dancers.*

Oh, well done, Denham. I've never seen you do that before. I shall have to learn that.

He turns to RICK.

You see, Rick, by giving them autonomy in certain areas and including them on aspects of running things they're forced to think, not only of themselves, but what's good for their class, the student body and ultimately the school.

RICK. Democracy in action.

MR FLORIAN. Exactly.

RICK. I see.

MR FLORIAN. I know your worry, Mr Braithwaite. But they can't vote away subjects – interesting idea though, we should put it up for discussion? Are you hungry?

He leads RICK *off while trying to emulate* DENHAM*'s dance move.*

Scene Four

We hear Chopin's 'Fantaisie-Impromptu'.

RICK *stands in front of the class. The* KIDS *sit at desks. Looking sullenly at him.*

RICK. Well, I thought that was a most interesting assembly.

Pause.

No one says anything. They just stare silently back at him. He turns and starts to write on the blackboard.

How interesting that the headmaster should use my favourite composer, Frederick Chopin. And John Keats, 'La Belle Dame Sans Merci'. A poem I too learned at school.

The blackboard now has 'John Keats 1795–1821'. Alongside 'Frederick Chopin 1810–1849'. He turns and looks back at the class. They are still staring at him.

Both renowned artists of the Romantic school. Does anybody know anything about the Romantic school?

The KIDS *continue to stare.* RICK *looks uncomfortable and puts down the chalk.*

DENHAM. Is it in Stepney?

RICK (*unsure how to take it*). Erm, no, what I mean is –

DENHAM. Then we wouldn't know anything about it. Would we?

Beat.

RICK. No – Well then...

MONICA PAGE. It's in Bromley-by-Bow. Three Mills – Near the brewery.

DENHAM. Naaah, it ain't.

RICK. Yes. Thank you... Now, the headmaster has told you my name, but it will be some little while before I know all of yours. So in the meantime, if I just point at you, I hope it won't be taken rudely.

MONICA PAGE. It's gotta be on the Whitechapel Road then.

RICK. It doesn't matter.

MONICA PAGE. Then why ask us? I've spent bleeding time thinking about it now, I have.

PAMELA DARE. Me too. I think it's on Brick Lane.

MONICA PAGE. By the synagogue?

PAMELA DARE. That's it.

RICK. It's really nothing that important. Now, I don't know anything about your abilities, so I'll begin from scratch. One by one I'll listen to your reading; so when I call out your name, will you please read anything you like from one of your school books.

RICK looks down at his register.

Erm... Denham?

He looks at the class. DENHAM *reluctantly stands. He's a surly-looking tough.*

DENHAM. Me, sir?

RICK. Could you start, please.

The GIRLS find him amusing.

DENHAM. What should I read?

RICK. Anything from one of your school books.

DENHAM. Which one?

MONICA PAGE. He's just said any bleedin' book, dummy!

DENHAM. He didn't ask you!

MONICA PAGE. I'd know what to bleedin' read if he did!

The others all laugh.

RICK. Thank you! Any book you have in your desk, Denham.

DENHAM *picks up the lid of his desk and looks.*

MONICA PAGE. Someone run down the bleedin' library for him, for God's sake!

RICK. Would you mind your language, please.

More laughter from the others. DENHAM *produces a book.*

DENHAM. I've got this.

He holds up a book.

RICK. That'll do. Please start reading.

DENHAM. 'In… I… g-ot… bod… illy… in… to the… app… le… baaaarel – barrel.'

RICK. Thank you, Denham. You can sit down now.

MONICA PAGE. That was worth the bleedin' wait.

RICK *looks at her.*

RICK. You seem to have a lot to say for yourself. Who might you be?

MONICA PAGE. Monica Page, sir. Should I read for you now, sir?

RICK. If you will, please.

She grabs at the book held by DENHAM.

MONICA PAGE. Gis' that –

DENHAM. Get your own.

RICK. It's *Treasure Island*, Monica. You should have your own copy.

She reaches into her desk, looks, and pulls out the book.

MONICA PAGE. This it?

RICK *nods his head.*

What page?

DENHAM. Fifty-three.

RICK. It's of no consequence.

MONICA PAGE. Fifty-three. Here we go.

MONICA PAGE *gives a sniff, pushes out her breasts and starts to read. And in a BBC* Watch with Mother *voice, says:*

Are you sitting comfortably? Then I'll begin.

RICK. Yes, thank you, Monica.

MONICA PAGE. 'InIgotbodilyintothebarreland-foundtherescarceanappleleft'

All the others start to laugh.

Get stuffed, you lot. At least I can read.

RICK. Thank you, Monica. You may sit down now.

MONICA PAGE (*pleased with herself*). I'm good, aren't I, sir?

RICK. Well, you read all the words, but didn't necessarily make any sense of them. A feat I doubt Robert Louis Stephenson himself could ever have imagined.

MONICA PAGE *looks to the class.*

MONICA PAGE. At least I read all the bleedin' words, you toerags.

There is sniggering coming from the back of the class, where some of the BOYS *are turning back to look at* DENHAM, *who is showing something around to them.* RICK *strides over and snatches the item from one of the* BOYS. RICK *looks at it. Realises what it is.*

DENHAM. Here, that's mine. Give us it back. You can't take that!

MONICA PAGE. Yeah, give it him back, sir.

RICK. If you insist on bringing such disgusting objects into school. You run the risk of having them confiscated.

DENHAM. It's the human body, sir. It's not disgusting, sir.

ROSE. Don't give it him back, sir. It's rude that is.

PAMELA DARE. I'll tell your mum you've got that, Denham.

MONICA PAGE. She's the one gave it to him.

They all laugh.

JANE PURCELL. No, that was 'is granny.

DENHAM. Me gran's the model!

SEALES. Jane Purcell's the model!

More laughter.

JANE PURCELL. Shut it, Seales, you coon!

DENHAM. You'd need more bleedin' ink than that pen's got to cover Purcell's knockers!

All the BOYS *and some of the* GIRLS *laugh.*

RICK. Thank you. You'll have this back at the end of the day, Denham. If I see it again in school, I will take it off you and dispose of it once and for all.

DENHAM. D'you find the female form disgusting, sir?

RICK chooses to ignore this remark. He reads out another name.

RICK. Seales?

DENHAM. Your dad wants you, Seales.

More sniggering. The mixed-race BOY *holds up his hand.*

RICK. If you will please, Seales.

MONICA PAGE. Page fifty-three, wasn't it, sir?

RICK. It doesn't matter.

MONICA PAGE. Fifty-three, Seales.

SEALES. 'In I got... bodily... into the bar... reland... found there s... c... arse... ly s... carse... ly...'

RICK. *Scarcely. Scarcely* – It means few. Less.

SEALES. 'And found... scarcely – an apple left.'

The lights slowly fade. They come up and RICK *is standing looking out of the window. Another* BOY *is reading as badly as the others.*

ARCHIE. 'In I got bodily – '

RICK (*irritated*). Maybe start from another part of the book?

MONICA PAGE. At least get us out of this bleedin' barrel, it's getting a bit crowded in here!

The class start to laugh.

No wonder there's no more bleedin' apples!

RICK. Sit down, please.

RICK *walks up and down the aisles.*

I take it you would all agree that this book was written in English, your language and that of your ancestors? After listening to you read I'm not so sure whether you are reading badly deliberately, or that you are unable to understand or express yourselves in your own language. However, it may be that I've done you the injustice of selecting the worst readers. Would anyone else like to read for me.

PAMELA DARE *raises her hand.*

And you are?

PAMELA DARE. Pamela Dare, sir.

RICK *gestures that she has the floor.*

PAMELA *takes out a different book.*

'Oh what can ail thee, knight-at-arms,
Alone and palely loitering?
The sedge has withered from the lake
And no birds sing.

> Oh what can ail thee, knight-at-arms,
> So haggard and so woe-begone?
> The squirrels's granary is full,
> And the harvest's done.
>
> I see a lily on thy brow
> With anguish moist and fever-dew,
> And on thy cheeks a fading rose,
> Fast withereth too.

RICK.

> 'I met a lady in the meads
> Full beautiful-a fairy's child,
> Her hair was long her foot was light,

PAMELA DARE.

> 'And her eyes were wild.'

Beat.

MONICA PAGE. What the bleedin 'ell was that?

RICK. 'La Belle Dame Sans Merci'... Thank you, Miss Dare.

The school bell goes and the KIDS *suddenly become animated as they grab coats and bags and head out of the classroom.*

Scene Five

RICK *sits at his desk. Head in his hands. There's a knock at the door.*

RICK. Come in.

CLINTY *comes in carrying two cups of tea. She places one in front of* RICK.

CLINTY. Thought you might need this.

She perches herself on the edge of his desk.

Well, how'd it go?

RICK *smiles and takes a sip of tea.*

RICK. Oh, not too badly. One of the boys was a bit of a nuisance. Denham, I think it was.

CLINTY. Yes, it would be. Testing the waters. He's the leader.

RICK. I took this pen from him. It's a got a woman and –

He passes it over to her.

CLINTY. I know, turn the pen upside down, the ink runs away revealing her gobstoppers. If only they'd show as much interest in pens that have ink on the inside. By the way, what's your name?

RICK. Braithwaite.

CLINTY. That what your parents called you, Braithwaite? 'Braithwaite, lunch is ready!' I hope you appreciate that I didn't attempt the accent!

RICK *smiles.*

RICK. Ricky or Rick, you know, short for Ricardo.

CLINTY. Mine's Vivienne, but everyone calls me, Clinty.

RICK. Clinty – It suits you. Sharp.

CLINTY. So I've been told.

RICK. I don't think I made much of a first impression on them.

She takes out a pack of cigarettes and lights up. Taking in the writing on the blackboard.

CLINTY. I don't know, Keats and Chopin? They're not going to forget that in a hurry. Did those dates come out of a book or did you have them stored in the old noggin?

RICK. The old noggin, I'm afraid.

CLINTY. Ouch!

RICK. But Clinty, the language they use and the... the smuttiness. I thought by showing them something of myself. My likes –

CLINTY. Nooooo!

RICK. What?

CLINTY. Never, never give of yourself so soon, at least not until they show an interest. Even then be wary or they'll find some way of using it against you.

RICK. You know it was easier trying to shoot down Messerschmitts.

CLINTY. Don't be so hard on yourself. We all know the old man's views and ideas about teaching, but it's us who have to put those theories into practice. And that, my dear, Ricky Ricardo, Braithwaite, is a different kettle of fish.

RICK. But am I expected to ignore it when I hear the way they speak to each other – to me?

CLINTY. Look at it from the kids' point of view, they come from homes where an order is invariably accompanied with a smack across the head. They might use bad language with their friends but they daren't try it at home, they'd get clobbered. So?

She looks at him pointedly.

RICK. So here they say and do anything they like without fear of any repercussions? And we're expected to accept it.

CLINTY. Precisely. So no matter how badly behaved they are, don't show it. Don't lay a finger on them, especially the girls or the next thing you know they'll be screaming high and low that you were interfering with them. But at the same time find some way of letting them know who's boss. We've all had to.

RICK. How did you show them?

CLINTY. I was born around hereabouts and they know it, so I can give as good as I get. It's a matter of finding your own balance... and theirs.

She looks up at the blackboard as she puts out her cigarette.

Keats and ruddy Chopin? Ohh, Ricky, Ricky, Ricky...

She takes up the teacups and heads out.

Scene Six

RICK *stands at the blackboard. He takes a second and begins to clean it off.*

DENHAM. You rubbin' off Chopin and Keats, sir? I thought you liked 'em?

MONICA PAGE. That's why he's rubbin' 'em off!

The KIDS *start to laugh.*

RICK. Our arithmetic lesson will be on weights and measures. As with our reading lesson, I am trying to find out how much you actually know so I can gauge how best to help you. So you can help me by answering questions as fully as you are able. Does anyone know the table weights of avoirdupois?

MONICA PAGE. 'Aver what?

DENHAM. I've had her.

MONICA PAGE. No you haven't, Denham. Ignore him, sir.

DENHAM. I've felt 'em!

NORA. Who hasn't.

MONICA PAGE. Shut it you, you scrubber!

NORA. Takes one to know one.

DENHAM. I've had her an' all!

NORA. In your dreams, Denham.

ARCHIE. In my dreams, actually!

> ARCHIE *grabs his cheeks and starts to pull on them making a wet, squelching sound. Some of the* GIRLS *scream out. This has the whole class in an uproar of laughter as other* BOYS *follow suit.*

RICK. Quiet down, please!

> *The classroom goes quiet as* RICK *stares them down.*

> Avoirdupois. It refers to those weights commonly used in grocers' shops and suchlike.

DENHAM. Yeah, I know.

> DENHAM *counts them off on his fingers.*

> Heavyweight, light-heavy, cruiserweight, middle, light bantam, flyweight, featherweight.

> *The others are impressed, clap and cheer him.* DENHAM *stands and takes a bow. He blows on his nails and polishes them on his chest.*

RICK. It's Denham, isn't it?

DENHAM (*mock surprise*). You've heard of me?

> *This has the others in fits.*

RICK. Well, Denham, that's one way of applying the table of weights. Are you interested in boxing, Denham?

> DENHAM *runs through a few muscleman poses, to the class's delight.*

DENHAM. I believe I can handle myself.

RICK. I see. Well, if you have at least learned to apply the table in that limited respect, it cannot be said that you are altogether stupid, can it, Denham.

> *There is a chorus of 'Oooooh!' from the class.*

MONICA PAGE. I think he's just been rude to you, Denham.

> *The laughter stops as they all turn to* RICK. DENHAM *gives him a dirty look.*

RICK. Is there anyone else who would like to say something about the table of weights?

A BOY at the back puts his hand up.

EDWARDS. Tons, hundredweights, quarters, pounds and ounces.

RICK. Yes. That's correct. What's your name?

EDWARDS. Edwards, sir. Edward Edwards.

DENHAM. They named him twice so he wouldn't forget.

RICK. Well, Edward Edwards, did you know that in places like the USA and the West Indies, although they use this same table of weights, they refer, to pounds or tons, but never to stones or hundredweights. So a man would speak of his weight as one hundred and seventy pounds, while here in England it would be twelve stone, two pounds which would put him at cruiserweight, wouldn't it, Denham?

DENHAM (*casual and authoritative*). Welterweight. God, who's the bloody teacher here?

The class laugh.

RICK. Thank you, Denham, welterweight. There are other weights in use. Troy weight is used by jewellers in weighing precious metals like gold, silver and platinum.

ESTHER JOSEPH. Diamonds are a girl's best friend, sir.

DENHAM. She's a Jew, so she should know. Probably got 'em stashed away all over the house.

FERNMAN. Shut it, Denham.

DENHAM. Oh, have I upset your girlfriend?

RICK. What did you mean by that remark, Denham?

DENHAM. What?

RICK. You referred to Miss Joseph, as a Jew who would know about diamonds.

DENHAM has no idea what RICK is talking about. He looks to the others.

DENHAM. It was a joke.

MONICA PAGE. Yeah, it was just a joke.

RICK. Two years ago the war ended. We are now in the process of trying members of the Hitler regime for the systematic murder of men, women and children, whose only crime was that they were Jews. The victims are now being numbered in their millions, do you think that's funny, Denham?

DENHAM *(surly and defensive)*. I didn't mean it like that, did I? – I just said –

RICK. That's how it begins, Denham… When people 'just say'. Don't let me hear you 'just say' it again. Any of you.

PAMELA DARE stands up and runs her fingers through a glass-bead necklace around her neck.

PAMELA DARE. Pearls is more my line, sir. Much more sophisticated, I think. A single string of pearls.

There is a chorus of 'Woooo!' 'Get her!' from the class.

DENHAM. Why didn't you say so, Pam. I've got a pearl necklace for you right here!

He grabs at his crotch and gives it a rub. Again, pandemonium.

RICK. I said enough!

RICK slams his book down on the desk. Everyone looks up at him.

I find it very interesting and encouraging to discover that you have a sense of humour, especially about something as simple and elementary as weights. As a matter of fact, you seem to find everything quite amusing. You were amused at your inability to read simple passages in your own language, and now you are amused at your own ignorance of weights. It is therefore clear to me that we shall have a delightful time together; you seem to know so very little, and are so easily amused, that I can looking forward to a very happy time.

The KIDS are unsure of what RICK has just said. There are a few murmurs of discontent.

MONICA PAGE. Are you allowed to say that to us?

RICK. Say what, Miss Page?

Beat.

MONICA PAGE. That what you just said then.

RICK. Let's turn our attention to measurements, beginning with
linear measurement. Do you know the table of linear
measurement – Denham.

DENHAM. Don't know what you mean.

RICK. Well, before I explain I'll wait till you've all had your
little laugh.

*He stands there looking expectantly at them as they glare
back at him.*

No? Nothing? Not even a giggle?... Well, it's called linear
because it deals with lines, inches, feet, furlongs and miles.

Scene Seven

RICK *is gathering up his books and putting them into his bag.*
MR FLORIAN *comes in.*

MR FLORIAN. Ahh, good, there you are, Mr Braithwaite. Glad
I caught you. Survived your first week. These are yours.

He hands RICK a sheaf of papers. End-of-the-week reports.
RICK *looks bemused.*

By the children. Reports on you. Other things as well, but
mostly about you and your teaching. They do them every
week.

RICK. Ah, yes. Miss Blanchard did mention them.

MR FLORIAN. The idea being that if something matters to the
child, he will go to great pains to set it down carefully and in
great detail.

RICK. I see.

MR FLORIAN. Stands to reason that it'll go towards improving their written English, spelling, construction and style. In turn, we get to see ourselves through the child's eyes… How we are perceived by them. Our behaviour. Whether what we teach is of any interest.

RICK. I…

MR FLORIAN. Yes?

RICK. I'm sorry, I don't quite follow, Headmaster. We're the teachers. They're here to learn from us.

MR FLORIAN. Yes?

RICK. What if they don't like what I teach?

MR FLORIAN. Then examine your methods.

RICK. You won't find a child in the world who doesn't dislike some aspect of schooling.

MR FLORIAN. There are some aspects of schooling I don't particularly like myself but it doesn't stop me from attending.

RICK. But you're the headmaster?

MR FLORIAN. And that makes me what?

RICK. That makes you… What I mean to say is, it's not necessary for you to…

MR FLORIAN. Yes?

RICK. You're here to teach, is what I'm saying. You're… you're the headmaster for starters – You're not here to learn.

MR FLORIAN. Aren't I? I disagree completely with that statement, Braithwaite. There's not a day goes by that I don't continue to grow and learn; from my classes, the other members of staff but particularly from the children. Teaching should be a continuous flow of ideas. We must never stop questioning ourselves and our relationship with the young people in that room. A child might not care much for something, Mr Braithwaite, but it doesn't mean they can't be engaged.

RICK. You think I should tailor my classes, because my class may not like the way I teach?

MR FLORIAN. No, but if they're all alluding to the same thing, we should be confident enough to accept that we might be failing them. Do you think so highly of your teaching that you believe every child is held in rapt attention by your methods?

RICK. Well no, but I believe –

MR FLORIAN. Teaching is hard, Mr Braithwaite. You can't just clock in and out. This isn't a factory, though there are plenty of individuals in the education department would have us think that way.

RICK. I think what I have to teach is important. If some of the kids find it boring, then... well, so be it. This is a school and they are here to learn. It's my job to teach them.

MR FLORIAN. Try to see them as individuals as well. If you can understand their individual needs, that would go a long way to knowing what they require as students.

RICK. I'm limited to a timescale. I barely have time to get through what I have now.

MR FLORIAN. Education has to be organic. We have to find a way to bring something different into the room. If we aren't excited by what we teach, how in God's name can we expect these children to feel inspired by what we have to say to them? It's all common sense, you know.

RICK. Common sense?

MR FLORIAN. Common sense. A simple phrase. An overworked phrase that seems to have lost all meaning in its flippancy of use, but is in fact the answer to so much, when applied in the right circumstances. Have a nice weekend, Braithwaite!

He walks off.

We hear: 'Listen While You Work' by Eric Coates, the theme from Workers' Playtime. *Lights fade and we hear the sound of a bus. Projected on the cyclorama we see a London as it journeys through the East End.*

Scene Eight

A bus seat has been placed on stage. RICK *is sat reading.*
GILLIAN *comes and sits next to him.*

GILLIAN. Morning, Rick.

RICK. Miss Blanchard, good morning.

GILLIAN. Gillian, please.

> *He stands politely and moves along the seat to allow her
> more space.*

Back for more, not put off by your first week, then?

RICK. I'm a glutton for punishment.

GILLIAN. That bad?

RICK. It was a trial by fire. But I was given some fine words of
advise from Clinty.

GILLIAN. Oh, taken you under her wing, has she?

RICK. It was a good place to seek refuge for a little while.

GILLIAN. Well, if you need another wing… Just come and
knock on my door.

RICK. Thank you. I will.

GILLIAN. How were your first reports?

RICK. Apart from the odd comment about having a new
'blackie teacher'… nothing. Certainly nothing that echoed
their behaviour in class.

GILLIAN. How was that?

RICK. Initially completely unresponsive to anything, but in a
strange way…

GILLIAN. Servile?

RICK. Precisely.

GILLIAN. They were just figuring out their strategy. Then they
became more aggressive, verbally challenging?

RICK. Yes. What should I expect next?

GILLIAN. It's hard to say. They've bypassed the silent treatment. With me it was 'Considering you're a bit of a toff, miss, your clothes don't look expensive – my nan's got a blouse just like that.'

RICK *laughs*.

What is it?

RICK. It's just all so far away from where I thought I'd be.

GILLIAN *looks quizzically at him as he continues to laugh*.

GILLIAN. Which was?

RICK. Before the war, I was a communications engineer. I specialised in new electronic technology.

GILLIAN. In England?

RICK. No, America.

GILLIAN. So how have you ended up here?

RICK. It's a long story, but basically it wasn't my ability that disqualified me from any of the jobs I sought…

GILLIAN. Oh.

RICK. Where as I was perfectly acceptable in Air Force Blue over Germany, it didn't have the same effect when applying for jobs that would place me above white Britons in the workplace.

GILLIAN. I'm so sorry. You must have felt terrible.

RICK. It brought me firmly back down to earth, so to speak.

GILLIAN. Oh, you must feel so angry. I would be. Damn angry.

RICK. Only with myself, for believing the war may have changed people's attitudes. It's hard when ideals die. But I won't allow it to beat me. I know who I am and what I can do and one day I'll get where I need to be.

GILLIAN. Good for you – Sorry, that sounded rather patronising. I mean –

RICK. I know what you mean. Thank you.

He looks out of the window.

This is us.

The sound of the bus stopping as the lights fade.

Scene Nine

Lights up on a darkened set. RICK *and* GILLIAN *walk on. A shadow ballet. The* STUDENTS *are paired off, kissing and groping with the hurried abandon of teenagers. Each couple break apart momentarily as they become aware of* GILLIAN *and* RICK, *but continue as they pass by.*

Scene Ten

The staffroom. RICKY *and* GILLIAN *enter.*

CLINTY. Morning, Ricky. Morning, Gillian.

WESTON *sees them and joins them.*

WESTON. Oh, I thought it was you two I saw getting off the bus together. Very cosy.

RICK. We've just witnessed the most – Well… On the stairwell. Some children were –

CLINTY. Weren't doing what children are supposed to do on Monday mornings. We know.

WESTON. I blame the rationing.

GILLIAN. There's nothing on ration down there, I can assure you.

CLINTY. I've seen a lot more than heavy petting in my time. Besides, they're hardly children, Mr Braithwaite. They know more about procreation than we ever did at their age.

WESTON. They probably witness the rutting rituals on a regular basis in the hovels they dwell in. Surely you should know that coming from your neck of the jungle. It's all on show over there, isn't it?

CLINTY. Oh, do shut up, Weston, you bearded buffoon. They're kids, Rick. We can't stop it. They'll only do it somewhere else. At least it's warm down there.

WESTON. And getting warmer by the minute, I shouldn't wonder.

RICK. But surely some decorum – decency –

CLINTY *starts to laugh.*

CLINTY. It's human nature, Rick. You can't fight it. It's inherent in the species. Men and women will look to each other.

WESTON. Although where you're from our four-legged friends haven't been left out of the equation by all accounts.

GILLIAN *and* CLINTY *both look at* WESTON *slightly horrified.*

GILLIAN. Oh, for goodness' sake, Mr Weston.

WESTON. I subscribe to the *National Geographic*. It's all in there.

CLINTY. I bet that's not all you subscribe to either.

WESTON. Scientific facts. Who am I to refute years of academic research?

GILLIAN. You do come out with the most utter... rot sometimes. Do you spend the whole night thinking up ways to be obnoxious?

WESTON. At last! The worm turns! I'm sorry, my dear, I seemed to have touched a raw nerve. I didn't know you were both – I mean to say that when I saw you both get off the bus together, I merely presumed that it was a happy coincidence.

GILLIAN. If you don't have anything civil to say. Then say nothing at all!

GILLIAN *heads out of the room.*

WESTON. I'd be careful there if I were you, old man.

RICK. I beg your pardon?

WESTON. Our Miss Blanchard. She's cocked a feather in your direction.

RICK. What on earth are you talking about, Weston?

WESTON. I think you've worked some of your black magic on her. I've never seen her so animated. Can't blame her though, strapping young buck like you...

He picks up his briefcase and heads for the door.

Still, no good will come of it. They never do, these things. Not part of nature's way, old man.

WESTON *leaves the room.*

CLINTY. Why don't you knock his bloody block off. No one would blame you.

RICK. That's exactly what he's daring me to do. Believe me, I've heard it all before.

CLINTY. He's right about one thing though.

RICK. And that is?

CLINTY. Gillian. She likes you.

RICK. And I her.

CLINTY (*exasperated*). Oh, Chopin and bloody Keats and he still hasn't got a clue! I said she likes you, likes you!

RICK. I find that hard to believe. It's such a short time... we hardly know each other.

CLINTY. Time's got nothing to do with it. It never has. It's an instant reaction. And believe me, she's had one.

RICK. Oh.

CLINTY. Oh? Oh? Is that all you've got to say, you silly man?

She leans in conspiratorially.

Listen, lose the Keats – I've got a copy of *Lady Chatterley's Lover* hot off the press.

RICK. Isn't that book illegal?

CLINTY. Nothing's illegal in this country, Rick, just as long as you don't do it in front of the vicar or Queen Mary.

The school bell goes.

Scene Eleven

RICK *stands with his back to the class copying from a book onto the blackboard. The class are copying what he is writing. There is a lot of whispering going on.*

RICK. Can you keep the noise down, please. You can't possibly be able to concentrate with that racket.

He carries on writing. He slides the board along and starts to rub out some of his previous work. There is a chorus of groans.

MONICA PAGE. Sir! I haven't finished that one yet!

PAMELA DARE. Me neither, sir.

DENHAM. You can't expect us to write it as quickly as you, sir.

RICK. As I said before, if you spent more time concentrating instead of chatting, you'd have got it finished. Those of you who haven't been able to finish. Stay in over lunch and copy it down at your own leisure.

SEALES. That's not fair, sir.

RICK. Life isn't fair, Seales.

PAMELA DARE. Sir, I'm just missing massive chunks.

RICK. Now, quietly put away your exercise books.

There is a clatter of desk lids and general noise.

I said quietly.

He takes a book down from a bookshelf.

I'm now going to read to you a poem by Rudyard Kipling. Some of you may know his work from *The Jungle Book* –

DENHAM. You'd know that one, Seales!

There is laughter from the KIDS.

RICK. Or the *Just So* stories. My personnel favourite is 'How the Elephant Got his Trunk'.

He looks to see if there is any reaction.

'How the Leopard got his Spots'? 'How the Camel got his Hump'?

MONICA PAGE. I'll be gettin' the bleedin' hump in a minute if I have to hear another bleedin' poem.

RICK *ignores her.*

RICK. The poem I'm about to read is called 'If'. A poem that continues to provoke debate amongst scholars of literature, as to its relevance on the life we live today. Whether its sentiments can be applied in the modern world. 'If' by Rudyard Kipling.

He clears his throat.

'If you can keep your head when all about you
Are losing theirs and blaming it on you,
If you can trust yourself when all men doubt you
But make allowances for their doubting too;

DENHAM *gives* MONICA PAGE *a nod.*

If you can wait but not be tired by waiting
Or lied about, don't deal in lies.'

MONICA PAGE *picks up her desk lid and lets it drop with a loud bang. It makes* RICK *spin round to see what the noise was.*

MONICA PAGE. Sorry, sir, It's this bleedin' lid. It's broke, sir.

RICK. You're meant to be listening. Not opening your desk.

He returns to the poem.

> 'If you can meet with triumph and disaster
> And treat those two imposters just the same;'

DENHAM *looks over at* FERNMAN.

DENHAM (*whisper*). Fernman…

He indicates his desk lid. FERNMAN *acknowledges him.*

RICK.

> 'Or watch the things you gave your life to broken – '

FERNMAN *drops the lid of his desk.*

RICK *looks up.*

Monica!

MONICA PAGE. It weren't my bleedin' fault, it was him.

FERNMAN. Sorry, sir, I just reached in for my ruler and the bloody thing fell down.

MONICA PAGE. Nearly took his bleedin' fingers off, didn't it?

RICK *ignores the sudden and deliberate use of curse words.*

RICK. Then I'll have a word about getting them fixed.

MONICA PAGE. Well, it's about bleedin' time if you ask me.

PAMELA DARE. Mines the bleedin' same, sir.

She lets hers drop with a bang.

DENHAM. And mine, sir.

He lets his drop.

RICK. Thank you, you can stop now.

ROSE. Mine's on its last bloody legs too, sir.

Soon the whole class are demonstrating their lid defects.

NORA. Mine's been like this since the bleedin' juniors.

He lets it drop again.

MONICA PAGE. It's a bloody cheek if you ask me. How do they expect you to work on these bleedin things, if they're all bleedin' knackered?

DENHAM. It's a bleedin' disgrace.

MONICA PAGE. I've a good mind to bleedin' report this to the bloody education people. You can't get a bleedin' education working on a bleedin' death trap like this. I could be crippled for bleedin' life, I could.

RICK. I said that's enough!

MONICA PAGE (*mock shock*). Bleedin'ell –

The class stop dropping the lids and turn to RICK.

RICK. What did you just say?

MONICA PAGE. What, sir? Me, sir?

RICK (*controlled*). You swore. You're always swearing. Does it make you feel any bigger or more intelligent to use such words in front of me? Am I supposed to feel shocked?

MONICA PAGE. Weren't just me!

RICK. I don't care. It is you I'm addressing. Tell me, is this the way you speak to your mother and father? Do you all address each other in this manner in this home. 'Here's your bleedin' tea, Dad.' 'Where's my bloody dinner?' 'Where's that bleedin' Monica?'

The other KIDS *are sniggering.*

Is that the way in which you communicate to each other?

MONICA PAGE. No, it's not!

RICK. Then why do you think I should put up with it in my classroom!

She looks about at the class. No one says anything. She turns back to look at RICK.

MONICA PAGE (*flat and vicious*). Because you're not my bleedin' dad!

The school bell rings and the KIDS *all jump up and head for the door.* RICK *sits down at his desk, as* MONICA PAGE, *looking triumphantly at him, is lead out by the others.*

As they exit we can hear: 'That put the black bastard in his place.' 'Cheeky bloody coon.' 'How dare he talk about my bleedin' parents like that?' 'Bloody monkey.' 'Good job he didn't try that on me.' 'You showed him there, Monica!'

Scene Twelve

The staffroom. RICK *is slumped in a chair. The others are sat about.* CLINTY *is laughing out loud.*

CLINTY. But Ricky, Kipling?! I thought we'd decided to abandon the nineteenth century?

RICK. I think the poem still has some points to make about the way we conduct ourselves as individuals.

CLINTY. Only if your name's Rupert and you want to go charging across the Somme, all colours flying!

GILLIAN. I think they reeled you in, Rick –

CLINTY. Hook, line and sinker, boyo.

GILLIAN. Did you get angry? Please, say you didn't?

RICK. I didn't show it.

CLINTY. Good. Thank heavens for small mercies. You're getting there, Rick.

RICK. Am I? It doesn't feel that way.

CLINTY. It's harder with your kids, Rick; there they are, about to leave and join the real world and already they're completely jaded. Don't be too hard on them. They mean no harm, really; they're not too bad when you get to know them.

RICK. How am I supposed to get to know them, if all they do is resist any efforts I make to help them?

WESTON *peers over his newspaper.*

WESTON. Why on earth does he need to know them?

GILLIAN. Really, Mr Weston, I think you should take a look at whether you're suited to working in a school like this.

WESTON. I didn't say the beggars shouldn't be educated. Lord knows you've got to have a basic education to work on a factory floor, these days. I just don't see what becoming their best friend will bring you – apart from possibly head lice and ringworm.

CLINTY. Bring back those dark satanic mills, eh, Weston?

WESTON. At least you'd be able to get a decent ruddy shirt off ration.

CLINTY. You carry on the way you're going, Rick.

GILLIAN. Yes, you're doing a splendid job. Don't be too downhearted.

RICK. Oh, I intend too.

WESTON. I thought you emancipated johnnies, were all against Kipling, anyhow. Imperial prop of Empire and all that.

RICK. I happen to think Kipling's work goes beyond Imperial politics.

CLINTY. He was a writer of his time and of his class.

WESTON. Not you as well –

RICK. Precisely, Clinty, and that's no reason to discount and condemn everything he wrote.

Beat.

WESTON (*feigning boredom*). Oh, God, I feel like slamming down my own 'bleedin'' desktop down.

RICK. I'm a product of the British Empire.

WESTON (*mock surprise*). You know, if you hadn't of pointed that out, old chap –

RICK. My ancestors' slavery was a product of it. This area where these children and their families have lived and made a living for generations, is a product of it too. The Empire, will have far-reaching consequences on this nation, long after it ceases to exist.

WESTON. What's that got to do with this lot? Waste of ruddy time if you ask me. Teach 'em the basics and send 'em off.

RICK. I happen to believe its history is pertinent to their development. How they see themselves as citizens of this country and its relationship with the people of its dominions. It's imperative that they understand all aspects of what made them and this wonderful country. Especially the Imperial props.

The school bell sounds and RICK *stands to leave.*

RICK.
       'Take up the White Man's burden –

CLINTY *and* GILLIAN *start to laugh.*

       Send forth the best ye breed –
       Go bind your sons to exile
       To serve your captive's need;'

WESTON. Are you taking the mickey?

RICK *heads for the door.*

RICK.
       'To wait in heavy harness
       On fluttered folk and wild –
       Your new sort sullen peoples,
       Half devil and half child.'

He exits to a cheer and a round of applause. Everyone laughing except WESTON.

WESTON (*flustered*). Well… There's no need to ruddy well encourage him!

This sends the WOMEN *into further fits of giggling.*

Scene Thirteen

RICK *enters the classroom. The room is filled with smoke. The* KIDS *are standing about joking and laughing.*

RICK. What the hell is going on here!

He pushes through the throng of KIDS *and looks at the fireplace.*

What is that?

SEALES. It's a ladies' whatsit. You know, sir... a thingamabob.

DENHAM. When they've got an oil leak down below in the engine room, sir.

DENHAM *points down to his crotch.* RICK *is disgusted by what he sees.*

There is sniggering behind him. He turns on the kids, fuming.

RICK. All of you boys out of the room now.

DENHAM. We haven't done anything.

RICK. Out, now!

The BOYS*, shocked at his anger, head off. The* GIRLS *start to follow.*

You girls stay behind.

The GIRLS *stop.*

Stand over there, all of you.

In the little while that I've been here I have become more and more dismayed at your general behaviour. Neither your deportment or grooming leaves me with any doubt that you care very much about your reputations, as you allow yourselves to be mauled about in public, like cheap dockside tarts. But this! I never thought I would meet women who were so lacking in dignity and self-respect, that they would permit themselves to be used in this disgusting manner.

ESTHER JOSEPH. But, sir –

RICK. I'm talking! There are certain things which decent women keep private at all times. Only a filthy slut would have dared to do this thing, and those of you who stood by and encouraged her are just as bad. I want that object removed and the windows open to clear away the stench.

The GIRLS *pick up the waste bin and scuttle out of the room.* RICK *opens his briefcase and starts to shove books into them. He begins to empty his desk.*

MR FLORIAN. Ah, Mr Braithwaite –

RICK. That's it! No more! I'm tired of their utter disrespect, the utter contempt… How am I supposed to engage with these monsters! Monsters, yes. That's exactly what they are. I'm sorry if that offends you, sir. But I've had enough! There isn't a spark of common decency in any of them. Everything they say or do is… is coloured with viciousness and filth. Why? If it's not because I'm black, then why? Do they want me to be another Hackman?

MR FLORIAN. You will be if you walk out on them now. You'll just be turning your back on them like most other adults in their lives.

RICK. I can only be their teacher.

MR FLORIAN. We have to be much more than that.

RICK. Is it my fault they're growing up in slums?

MR FLORIAN. No it isn't. And that's not what I'm saying.

RICK. Then what are you saying? That I should just grin and bear it? I've been walking into that room every day for months now and –

MR FLORIAN. And you still haven't a clue who they are.

RICK. I've tried… I am trying desperately to understand them. But you expect me to throw everything I've ever learned, about how one conducts oneself, out of the window? There has to be some form of mutual respect in the classroom.

MR FLORIAN. No. You walk into that room and you already see yourself as being morally and intellectually superior to them. Don't you think they see that you're teaching?

RICK. I'm their teacher!

MR FLORIAN. It doesn't mean anything. If you walk in there wearing your cloak of authority. Demanding respect because you think you're something special, then they will fight back. I'm glad they fight back. At least it shows they still have some fight left in them.

RICK. I just… I don't understand what it is you want me to do? I go in there and I feel that I'm failing every day. Failing them, and that's not what I want. I just end up spewing out facts and figures and it means nothing – to them and to me!

MR FLORIAN. It's not just you, the whole system's rotten. We need a bloody revolution, followed by an equally bloody civil war! We need to be radical. There's too much at risk for the future. For the way we want society to develop. It must start now. Here. With you and those children in your classroom.

RICK (*despondent*). I know nothing. Nothing about them. About teaching! I haven't a clue really, have I? I haven't got a bloody clue about any of this! And these useless bloody things! Have taught me nothing!

RICK o*pens his briefcase and shakes out his books.*

MR FLORIAN. Let's burn the bloody books! Burn, foul and vicious lies! Burn in the bottomless pits of hell! Oh, Mr Braithwaite, this is your Damascene moment! Feel it! Enjoy it! Bask in its light!

RICK *picks up his books and tosses them into the fire. Smoke starts to rise. He starts to whoop and dance about the room.*

I told you, Rick, there are no blueprints to this job. Now you will rise phoenix-like from the ashes. You are reborn, no longer a virgin. You will go forth and communicate. The shackles of established teaching methods lay broken at your feet.˙

RICK. How can I possibly speak to them, when I don't know them.

MR FLORIAN. Well, now it's time to find out!

RICK. You know something? They don't know me either.

MR FLORIAN. Exactly!

RICK. Ohh, but they're going to! I know how to conduct myself! How to behave civilly to people.

MR FLORIAN. Yes!

RICK. How to show respect, where respect is due.

CLINTY comes in.

MR FLORIAN. See! He walks!

There's smoke coming from the smouldering books.

CLINTY. What's all this smoke?

MR FLORIAN. We have a Pope!

RICK. No more 'bleedin'' and 'bloody', no more banging desks. And silence! I'll have that too. Silence on demand. They've pushed me about as far as I'm willing to go. Now I'll do a bit of pushing of my own!

He heads out of the room. MR FLORIAN *collapses happily onto the sofa.*

Beat.

MR FLORIAN. Rick seems to be settling in nicely?

ACT TWO

Scene One

RICK *stands in front of the class.*

RICK. Good morning, class. As your teacher, I think it right and proper that I should let you know something of my plans for you.

He looks about the class. They say nothing but stare back at him.

My... my purpose in being here is to teach you and I shall do my best to make it as interesting as possible in what little time we have left together. If at any time I say something which you do not understand or with which you do not agree, I would be pleased if you would let me know.

Beat.

I'm going to, with your help, restructure the work we do here together. I want us to discuss your future. About what happens after you leave us this summer. Your hopes, dreams, the practicalities of looking for employment. From now you will be treated, not as children, but as young men and women.

As he says 'women' he looks directly at the GIRLS, *who all look rather sheepish.*

Both by me and each other.

Suddenly, MONICA PAGE *bursts in and sits down in her seat. She pulls out a textbook and lets her desk slam back down. Everyone looks at her. Then back to* RICK, *waiting for him to explode.* RICK *casually walks over to the door.*

For instance, there are really two ways in which a person may enter a room –

He opens the door.

One is in a controlled, dignified manner, the other is as if someone has planted a heavy foot in your backside. Miss Page has just shown us the second way; I'm sure she will now give us a demonstration of the first.

Everyone looks at MONICA PAGE.

Well, Miss Page?

MONICA PAGE, *unsure, gets up and walks to the door, opens it and steps out closing it behind her. Moments later the door opens and she comes back through gently closing the door behind her and goes back to her seat.*

Thank you, Miss Page. As from today there will be certain courtesies that will be observed at all times in this classroom. Myself you will address as Mr Braithwaite or sir – the choice is yours. The young ladies will be addressed as miss and the young men will be addressed by their surnames.

SEALES. Why should we call them miss, when we know them... sir.

RICK. Is there any young lady here you consider unworthy of courtesies, Seales?

All the GIRLS *turn to look at* SEALES *as if daring him to say anything.* SEALES *is unnerved by them.*

SEALES. Erm, no, sir...

The GIRLS *turn back to* RICK.

RICK. I've already made clear my pertinent points to the ladies last week. I will add that in the future they must show themselves both worthy and appreciative of the courtesies we men will show them. As Seales said, we know you. We shall want to feel proud to know you, and just how proud we shall feel will depend entirely on you. Now, gentlemen, there is nothing weak and unmanly about clean hands and faces, and shoes that are polished. A real man never needs to prove himself in the way he dresses or cuts his hair. Being a real man has nothing to do with muscle, fists and knifes. You have it in you to be a fine class, the best this school has ever known. But it is entirely up to you now. I am here to help, but ultimately the responsibility is on you. Now, are there any questions?

MONICA PAGE *puts up her hand.*

RICK. Yes, Miss Page?

MONICA PAGE. What about Mr Weston, sir? He's never tidy and he's always picking his nose when he thinks you're not watching him.

RICK. Mr Weston is a teacher, Miss Page, and we shall not discuss him.

There is a murmur of discontent.

I am your teacher, and I'm the one you should criticise if I fail to maintain the standards I demand of you.

The school bell goes. But the KIDS *continue to sit. Neither* RICK *or they know quite why there hasn't been the sudden rush for the door.*

Beat.

That'll be all for now. Thank you for listening.

They slowly rise and begin to gather up their things and head out of the door. As the door closes, RICK *slumps back into his chair. A look of surprise on his face. As the lights fade we hear 'Hole in the Wall' by Albina Jones.*

Scene Two

The KIDS *are jiving away, watched by* GILLIAN. RICK *comes in and joins her.*

GILLIAN. I was never very good at this. I think it has something to do with a middle-class upbringing and an abject fear of showing my knickers in public.

RICK. And that's precisely what I want to ask you about?

GILLIAN. Flashing my unmentionables?

RICK. Could I ask a favour of you, Gillian?

GILLIAN. Ask away.

RICK. I told the girls in my class that you'd give them some tips on deportment, how to dress well and make-up.

GILLIAN. You said what?

RICK. It's one area of expertise I don't have, I'm afraid.

GILLIAN. What on earth are you talking about?

RICK. Let's get out of here.

They head into the corridor and walk towards the staffroom.

They want to start looking their best.

GILLIAN. And they said this to you? Apropos of nothing?

RICK. Well, not quite. You see... I told them they all looked and acted like dockside tarts.

GILLIAN. You said what?

RICK. It's a long story, but in short, they asked me how they were supposed to look. And I gave you as an example.

GILLIAN *starts to laugh.*

GILLIAN. Very well, count me in. They couldn't do any worse, I suppose. At least my sojourn at an expensive finishing school won't have been a complete waste of time.

RICK. Thank you, Gillian. You've saved my neck.

GILLIAN. How's it all going?

RICK. Well – I think. I'm trying to look at things differently…
My approach. I feel they're beginning to trust me a little.

GILLIAN. Really?

RICK. Well, they're speaking to me.

GILLIAN. That's always a good sign.

RICK. More importantly, I'm getting to know them a little more.

GILLIAN. But that's wonderful, Rick.

RICK. It's just Denham.

GILLIAN. It's always Denham.

RICK. He's antagonistic. He's the one pulling all the strings. I
don't think he's bullying them. That's just it, they all seem to
like and support each other in an odd way. But Denham…
he's the natural leader of the group and for some reason he's
resistant to me.

GILLIAN. Resistant to the charms of Rick Braithwaite? How
dare he.

RICK. They're good kids, Gillian. I didn't see it at first. Some
of them have a real thirst for knowledge. But their
expectations in life are so low.

GILLIAN. What else would you expect, growing up here?

RICK. It's not just that. It's as if… I don't know… They don't
have any dreams. It's assumed these kids are incapable of
achieving anything. The terrible thing is they believe it
themselves.

GILLIAN. There are lots of people from similar backgrounds
who've done very well for themselves, in all walks of life.

RICK. I bet they weren't encouraged to think that way in
school. We have to change that. We have to change the way
we communicate with them.

GILLIAN. Rick, I talk to these kids every day.

RICK. We don't – we don't, Gillian, we walk in and we start
laying down the law of learning. Life is a struggle. That's what

we should be telling them. You have to struggle for what you want. But they need to believe that things are possible.

GILLIAN. We're worlds apart from them. No matter how much we care.

RICK. We're not.

GILLIAN. Oh, Rick –

RICK. The only thing these kids lack, that we had, is ambition. They need to be aware that there are possibilities. We shouldn't encourage them to sit back and be content with mundane lives working in a shop or on the docks or on the market –

GILLIAN. What's wrong with that, if they're happy?

RICK. Nothing. Nothing at all. I just want them to know that there are other choices. Yes, we teach them how to read, write and count, but... It has to be more than that. There has to be much more to teaching than that. They have to understand that life is important – their lives are important, that their contribution to life will be equally important. We have to tell them about the world that exists out there. A world and opportunities that are there for everyone.

GILLIAN. And from what you've experienced – are they there for everyone?

RICK. Yes. I believe they are. I have to believe they are for my own sake as well as theirs.

GILLIAN. It's a lovely idea. But most of them won't go further than the end of their streets.

RICK. Fine. Then I'll walk to the end of the street with them and tell them what else there is to see around the corner.

GILLIAN. I see Mr Florian's made a convert.

Beat.

RICK. It's just common sense.

GILLIAN. What?

RICK. Nothing, just something someone said to me once.

Scene Three

RICK *stands at the front of the class. There is a large object under a dust sheet beside him. The* KIDS *are intrigued by it. Suddenly, with a dramatic flourish, he pulls off the cover. Hanging from a stand is a laboratory skeleton. Some of the* GIRLS *and a couple of the* BOYS *scream. Then they start laughing and making fun of it.*

DENHAM. Cor blimey, he's gone and brought his dinner in.

> *All, apart from* DENHAM, *are dressed smarter and are more groomed.* RICK *accepts the laughter and the jokes.*

RICK. Alright, if you would all just settle down.

DENHAM. That your girlfriend, sir?

> *The others laugh.* RICK *smiles good-naturedly.*

RICK. Certainly not, Denham. As you should all know by now I wouldn't take out a lady so, inappropriately dressed.

> *All except* DENHAM *laugh.*

MONICA PAGE. That's funny that, sir, I didn't know youse could make jokes that I could laugh at.

PAMELA DARE. Why shouldn't he?

RICK. Is there anything you'd like to ask me about this skeleton?

DENHAM. Was she tasty?

RICK. She? Why do you presume it's a woman, Denham?

DENHAM. It ain't got nothin' between its legs, has it!

RICK. And nor would it, Denham. The penis is an organ and not a bone. It would have rotted away long ago. But you're right, this is the skeleton of a female.

PAMELA DARE. How can you tell, sir?

DENHAM. It won't shut up talking!

> *There is good-natured laughter.*

RICK. Because the female pelvis is wider, for childbirth. The male is much narrower.

MONICA PAGE. My mum's must be huge, sir, there's ten of us!

More laughter.

EDWARDS. Blimey, I'm surprised she can keep anything in at that rate.

They all laugh.

DENHAM. What colour was she then?

PAMELA DARE. Denham!

RICK. No, Miss Dare. Denham has a point. How can we tell what race a skeleton is? Well, race is best identified by the skull. Caucasians have angled, gently sloping eye sockets and triangular nasal cavities. The Negro has a much more rectangular eye socket and a smaller, squatter nasal cavity. Asians typically have an oval-shaped nasal cavity and wider eye sockets.

DENHAM. What's she, then?

RICK. She was white.

DENHAM. Oh, right, then she can't be your girlfriend then, eh. Then again, it could be Seales' mum!

SEALES. Shut it.

DENHAM. You gonna shut it for me?

SEALES *says nothing.*

PAMELA DARE. I think she looks sad, sir.

DENHAM. What d'you expect, she ain't eaten for years!

MONICA PAGE. I think she should be in the ground. Proper burial. Decent like. It's not right, sir.

SEALES. Then how could we learn about skeletons and that, Miss Page?

RICK. A good point... Did you know doctors and surgeons used to have grave robbers steal bodies so that they could study and discover more about human anatomy?

SEALES. Like Burke and Hare, sir?

RICK. Exactly.

The class are fascinated.

MONICA PAGE. That's not right.

RICK. Do you know something else I know about this woman?

He produces a pipe from his pocket and sticks it in the skeleton's mouth.

She smoked a pipe.

They all start to laugh. RICK *too.*

It's true. Look here.

He points to her teeth.

You see here, this gap between the upper and lower plates. How the teeth are worn down. That is through the constant use of a pipe being placed in that position. She probably smoked from a very early age. Like you.

There are murmurs of awe at this information as various KIDS *examine the gap.*

So tell me. What do we know about this woman, so far?

PAMELA DARE. She was white.

SEALES. Of child-bearing age, sir.

RICK. What about her social standing.

MONICA PAGE. Her what, sir?

RICK. Was she a toff?

MONICA PAGE. Not smoking a blee–… I mean a pipe, sir.

SEALES. And she's small, sir. That's caused through not eating well, sir.

RICK. Correct, Seales. Bad dietary habits. Anything else?

DENHAM. She's bald.

The KIDS *laugh loudly.*

RICK. And…

Beat.

PAMELA DARE. She's one of us, isn't she, sir?

The KIDS *stop laughing and look to* PAMELA.

RICK. Yes, Miss Dare. One of you. Or rather how one of you
ladies may have been over a hundred years ago.

The GIRLS *go quiet.*

This skeleton came from the London Hospital, just down the
road. She was probably a native of this area. She's in her
teens. From her size we can see she was probably
malnourished. She has poor teeth. She smoked a pipe, which
also tells us that she wasn't ever going to be having tea with
Queen Victoria. We'll never know how she ended up like
this. Maybe she was a derelict.

MONICA PAGE. I wonder what she looked like. You know,
with skin and that? What colour her hair was?

SEALES. What do you think her name was, sir?

DENHAM. How the hell does he know, you berk.

RICK. We'll never know. But it was quite common for people of
her period to use the names of members of the Royal Family.

PAMELA DARE. Yeah! My grandmother was named Victoria,
sir. Like the Queen.

MONICA PAGE. My granddad was called, Edward, sir.

RICK. After Queen Victoria's eldest son. Edward Prince of
Wales. Who later became?

MONICA PAGE. King Edward the seventh, sir. He came to the
East End, sir, my granddad saw him.

Beat.

DENHAM. My gran was called, Albert.

RICK *ignores* DENHAM.

RICK. So you see, from merely looking at this one skeleton, we
can learn not only about our own anatomy, but discover so
much about our past and our social history as well.

PAMELA DARE. What do you think she wore, sir?

RICK. Well, why don't you take out your copies of *Oliver Twist*.

There is a chorus of moans from the KIDS.

I was about to say – and just look at the illustrations.

Excitedly they all open their desks and grab their books.

They're exactly the kind of clothes this young lady and you would probably have worn.

PAMELA DARE. I'd have loved to wear a big dress like that, sir.

RICK. I'm sure you would have looked very elegant in it, Miss Dare.

PAMELA DARE. Do you think so, sir, really?

RICK. I'm sure.

SEALES. I'd of liked a top hat like the Artful Dodger, sir.

The other KIDS *laugh.*

RICK. You should go along to the Victoria and Albert museum. They have a wonderful display of costumes there.

MONICA PAGE. Us, sir?

PAMELA DARE. Go to a museum on our own?

RICK. But why wouldn't you? It's not very far. South Kensington.

DENHAM. It wouldn't happen. We don't go to places like that.

PAMELA DARE. Couldn't you take us, sir?

RICK *is unsure how to respond to this.*

SEALES. Yeah, sir. We could go with you.

The others except DENHAM *join in the plea.* RICK *looks at them.*

DENHAM. Well, sir? Are you gonna take us then?

RICK *looks at them.*

RICK. Well, I could certainly put it to the headmaster. It's worth a try. He can only say no.

The KIDS *cheer.* DENHAM *gives* RICK *a dirty look.*

DENHAM. One other thing.

RICK. Yes, Denham.

DENHAM. Regarding clothes and that. We've got this book at home and it's got blacks in it dancing about with nothing on. My gran says they're all 'bare-arsed where they come from'. Are your parents like that?

All the KIDS *look at* RICK *as he is challenged to respond by* DENHAM.

RICK. I think what your Granny Albert, is referring to, Denham –

The other KIDS *laugh at this joke.*

RICK *smiles.*

Is that some people in very hot climates prefer to wear next to nothing. Which may seem odd to us and our customs but is perfectly natural to them. As for my parents? Well, they both studied at Cambridge, so I would have thought it rather chilly to be wandering about its precincts totally naked. Besides, my family come from British Guyana where the custom is to be fully clothed at all times, unless of course you're in the bath.

The other KIDS *laugh at this. The school bell goes and the kids head out in high spirits.* GILLIAN *heads into the classroom.*

GILLIAN. They're happy about something.

RICK. I want to take them on a trip.

GILLIAN. Really, where?

RICK. The V&A, to see the costume exhibition.

They enter the staffroom.

Scene Four

The staffroom.

WESTON *is sat reading the paper.*

CLINTY *is sat drinking tea and reading and smoking a cigarette.*

GILLIAN. Goodness, are you sure you want to do that?

CLINTY. Do what?

RICK. Take my children on a field trip.

WESTON. Good God, have you brought your family over here already?

As usual RICK *ignores him.*

RICK. What do you think, Clinty?

CLINTY. I don't think the old man will allow it. But I think it's a great idea.

RICK. Good for you, Clinty.

WESTON. You want to lead the great unwashed into the real world? Don't we have to give a year's notice for something like that? So they can screw everything down.

RICK. I think it would be interesting for them to see some of the things we've been talking about in class.

WESTON. God protect us from reformers. I swear this is missionary zeal in reverse! Leave them alone, man, we like our working class as they are. Two world wars have already given them strange notions of equality as it is.

CLINTY. Oh, do shut up, Weston. Where're you thinking of taking them, Rick?

RICK. The Victoria and Albert museum.

WESTON. All of them?

RICK. All of them, Weston. Fancy joining us?

WESTON. Rather tear off my own testicles, old boy.

CLINTY. I think they'll have a wonderful time, Rick.

WESTON. Are you going to be able to manage them?

RICK. I manage them here, don't I?

WESTON. I dare say you do. But this will be very different.
Like taking the Mongol hordes to the Ballets Russes.

RICK. That's a wonderful idea, Weston – the ballet, I hadn't
thought of that. Maybe if this trip goes well.

WESTON. You're doomed. There's going to be rape and pillage
the likes of which have not been seen in London since the
Vikings! Lock up your daughters and your livestock, here
comes Green Slade School!

MR FLORIAN *comes in*.

RICK. Headmaster, just the man I want to see. I wondered if it
would be possible for me to take my class on a field trip.

MR FLORIAN *looks at* RICK.

MR FLORIAN. Outside the school?

RICK (*puzzled*). Yes.

MR FLORIAN. With your class?

RICK. Yes.

MR FLORIAN. How far are we talking?

RICK. South Kensington.

MR FLORIAN (*dramatically horrified*). 'But there be dragons
there, Rick!'

RICK *smiles*.

I wouldn't advise it, Rick. I'm not saying never. You're
settling in nicely but taking them across London on your
own is another matter altogether.

RICK. I'd like to try nonetheless.

MR FLORIAN. I'll tell you what, if you can persuade another
member of staff to accompany you –

GILLIAN (*enthusiastically*). I'll go.

> *Everyone turns to her.* CLINTY *smiles enigmatically and slips* RICK *a sly wink.*

MR FLORIAN….I'll say yes.

RICK. Would you, Gillian?

GILLIAN. Yes. I'd love to.

MR FLORIAN. There it is then. Permission granted. Good luck and Godspeed. Just get me a list of names and the date you intend to travel on and we'll hit the school funds for tickets and tuck!

WESTON. The Geneva Convention applies to all prisoners.

> MR FLORIAN *heads out of the room.*

CLINTY. Well done, Rick. Now, plan it carefully down to the minutest detail. Logistical ramifications and all that. Leave nothing to chance. Think of yourself as General Eisenhower on D-Day.

WESTON. Let's just hope it's not Dunkirk.

> *The lights slowly fade as Vera Lynn sings 'White Cliffs of Dover'.*

Scene Five

Victoria and Albert Museum.

We project interiors of the V&A on the stage.

RICK *enters wearing a rain mac, he is followed by* GILLIAN *and the* KIDS, *the class have really pushed the boat out on dressing for the occasion – all, that is, except* DENHAM. *They all look very excited a little bit nervous and awed.*

MONICA PAGE. God, it's full of toff kids, isn't it, sir?

RICK. You have every right to be here as well, Monica.

PAMELA DARE. I haven't heard anyone talkin' like me, sir.

RICK. So what? You're all well behaved and well turned-out all of you. My goodness but you all look very smart. I'm very proud to be here with you today. You make me look good.

They all smile at this acknowledgement of their efforts.

PAMELA DARE. You look very smart and handsome too, sir.

RICK. Thank you, Pamela.

PAMELA DARE. I feel a bit scared here, sir. Could I walk about with you.

RICK. There's no need for any of you to feel intimidated.

SEALES. It's a public museum, Miss Dare. Isn't it, sir?

RICK. That's right. Okay, quiet a moment, please; you all have paper and pencils. I want you to go and explore. Note down what you find especially interesting so we might talk about it later back at school. If in the event we become separated, we'll meet back here at 12 p.m.

DENHAM. What if I don't find anything interesting, sir?

RICK *takes a moment.*

RICK. Then you won't have to write anything down, will you, Denham?

DENHAM. I'll be bored.

RICK. Yes, you will, won't you. Now, just be aware that other people are here enjoying the museum as well as you. So let's respect that and keep the noise down to a minimum. Well, what are you waiting for? Go, enjoy yourselves.

The class scatters excitedly about the stage. Images of the exhibits are projected. Not only the costumes but exhibits from all over the world.

GILLIAN. Do you think that's wise, letting them wander off like that?

RICK. I shouldn't think they'll get into too much trouble.

GILLIAN. They like you, Rick. You're good with them.

RICK. They're growing on me.

GILLIAN. I think Pamela Dare has a real crush on you.

RICK *laughs*.

RICK. For heaven's sake, Gillian.

GILLIAN. She's no child, Rick. She's almost a woman. It's quite common. I dare say a few of my juniors are taken with me – I hope they are – I should be very disappointed if they weren't.

She smiles.

But Pamela, I would definitely say, has fallen in love with you.

RICK. It had never even crossed my mind.

GILLIAN. Of course it hadn't. I had a crush on my art teacher at school, for years. And believe me I played out every romantic scenario in the book. You know, he never so much as gave me a second glance.

RICK. But I haven't done anything to encourage it – I mean –

GILLIAN. You didn't need to. Look at the rest of the men we have in school. Mr Florian, Weston. Then along comes Mr Rick Braithwaite. Kind, generous, smartly dressed, big broad and handsome.

RICK. Really, Gillian.

GILLIAN. You've shown her respect. I can hear it when she talks about you. 'Sir said this.' 'Sir said that.' Just be patient

with her, Rick, she's only just finding out she's a woman.
You're turning out to be her ideal man.

RICK. It just never occurred –

GILLIAN. I feel sorry for any other man who comes along and
doesn't live up to your standards. They won't stand a chance
with her. Do you know something else, Rick?

RICK. What's that?

GILLIAN *moves closer to him.*

GILLIAN (*smiling*). I completely agree with her.

RICK. Oh?

GILLIAN. In fact, I find myself to be a little bit jealous.

*There is a moment when it looks as though they are about to
kiss. Suddenly they become aware that* SEALES *is standing
there watching them.*

RICK. Yes, Seales?

SEALES. I was just wondering if I could ask you something, sir.

RICK. Yes, Seales.

SEALES *looks at* GILLIAN, *she takes the hint.*

GILLIAN. I'll just go and see how the others are getting on.

She walks off.

RICK. What is it you wanted to ask me?

SEALES. I... I was watching you, sir, with Miss Blanchard, sir.

RICK. Yes.

Pause.

SEALES *looks as if he's about to change his mind as to what
he is about to ask.*

What is it, Seales?

SEALES. Do you think that it's okay... For a black man and a
white woman to be together, sir?

RICK *did not expect this.*

RICK. I… don't understand what you mean, Seales…

SEALES. It don't matter, sir…

He turns to go back to the others.

RICK (*unsure where this is leading*). Your mother's white, isn't she, Seales?

SEALES. Yes, sir. My dad's from Nigeria, sir.

RICK. Then I'm not sure what you want to know, Seales.

SEALES. It's what people say, sir. About me mum, sir.

RICK. Your parents' relationship has nothing to do with anyone else but them. Has someone said something in school to you?

SEALES. No, sir… Me mum's gone into hospital, sir. Some woman in the next bed saw me and my dad when we went to visit her, sir… She said it was unnatural – inhuman, that it made her want to throw up.

RICK *is angry and unsure what to say.*

RICK. Do you think it's unnatural for two human beings to love each other, Seales?

SEALES. No, sir.

RICK. Then that's all that matters. The world is full of such narrow-minded, bigoted people, Seales. They seem to have already forgotten that we fought a world war to bring an end to such philosophies. You can fall in love with whoever you damn well please and if anyone says anything to the contrary, you tell them to go to hell!

SEALES. Yes, sir.

RICK. Women like your mother are very special, Seales. Always remember that. They put up with a lot. Your father is a very lucky man to have found her.

SEALES. Thank you, sir, I think he knows that.

RICK. Good for him. Now, go on, off you go and join the others.

GILLIAN *comes back over. They both stand looking slightly embarrassed.*

GILLIAN. What's the matter, Rick?

RICK. Nothing.

GILLIAN. Was it because of what I said? I'm sorry, I just
wanted to –

RICK. You don't have to explain anything.

GILLIAN. I do have a tendency to run off at the mouth. Just
jump in, it was stupid of me – Sorry – Oh, I have spoilt it
now… Don't be angry with me –

RICK. Far from it. I'm glad you brought it up.

GILLIAN. Let's just pretend that I didn't say anything.

RICK. I don't want to do that either.

GILLIAN. Really? Nor do I.

RICK. But you know this kind of thing isn't easy.

GILLIAN. I think I know what I'm letting myself in for.

RICK. Do you?

GILLIAN. Does it matter?

RICK. You see, I've been in this situation before.

GILLIAN. Then I shan't feel so alone.

RICK. I hope not… Come on, we'd better go and find those kids.

Scene Six

The gym.

The BOYS *come running on in their gym kits, pushing a wooden vaulting horse. They stand around* ARCHIE, *as* DENHAM *ties his arm up in a sling.* FERNMAN *stands by the door.*

ARCHIE. Oh, come on, Denham, this isn't fair.

DENHAM. Shut it! No one asked your opinion.

SEALES. He's right, though, Denham. You could hurt him.

DENHAM. Remember whose side you're on, Seales. That goes for the rest of you and all. I'm gonna teach that wog a lesson he won't forget. He's got it coming.

FERNMAN. He's here!

They all line up as RICK *comes in. He has removed his shirt and is wearing a vest.*

RICK. Okay, let's start up with a bit of running on the spot.

DENHAM. Please, sir, could we do some boxing, sir? We never do any with Mr Weston, sir. He always makes us do the vaulting.

RICK. Very well, get the gloves and sort yourself out into pairs.

DENHAM. My partner's hurt his hand, sir?

DENHAM *points out* ARCHIE's *arm.*

Will you have a go with me, sir.

RICK. You can wait and have a bout with Potter or one of the others.

DENHAM. They'll be knackered, sir. I don't mind having a knock-about with you.

ARCHIE. Go on, sir, take him on!

FERNHAM. Yeah, there's nothing of him, sir!

RICK. No, Denham, you'll have to skip it for today.

DENHAM. You're not scared of me, are you, sir?

DENHAM *looks at the others. The others look at* RICK, *as if he chickened out. Even the ones who were against the fight initially.* RICK *realises he can't not fight* DENHAM *now.*

RICK. Very well, Denham. Put your gloves back on.

DENHAM *smiles at* POTTER *who slips the gloves back onto* DENHAM'*s hands.*

DENHAM *turns and starts dance over to* RICK, *who has taken a defensive position. They act out a few moves.* DENHAM *shows how he outclasses* RICK *with a few body blows. The rest of the lads are egging on both boxers.* DENHAM *lets* RICK *have another series of blows to the upper body. Again* RICK *reels backwards.*

SEALES. Come on, sir, go after him!

Suddenly, DENHAM *hits* RICK *squarely in the mouth.*

ARCHIE. Keep your guard up, sir!

RICK *has blood coming from his mouth. He looks at it and heads back to* DENHAM. DENHAM *attempts another volley of blows, but leaves himself open and* RICK *seizes the opportunity and sends a punch right in the stomach.* DENHAM *drops to the ground immediately, coughing.*

FERNMAN. Bleedin' 'ell!

SEALES. He's Joe Louis! The Black Bomber himself!

RICK. Potter, help him up. Seales, collect up the gloves. You others start running on the spot.

The others suddenly jump to the running on the spot. RICK *slips the gloves off his hands and goes over to* DENHAM.

Come along, Denham, you must have taken plenty of punches like that. I just got in a lucky shot.

DENHAM. No it wasn't, you're good. You got me good and proper.

RICK. Take yourself off to the washroom and soak your head. You'll feel much better afterwards.

DENHAM. Yes, thank you, sir.

RICK. Fernman, go with him.

Scene Seven

Staffroom.

RICK *is standing talking to* CLINTY. WESTON *is sat in his usual chair reading the newspaper.* GILLIAN *comes in. She goes over and casually puts her arm across* RICK*'s back.* WESTON *sees this and gives his newspaper a shake.*

GILLIAN. Rick, my parents are expecting us at the weekend.

RICK. Lovely, I look forward to it.

CLINTY. Are you going to Pangbourne?

GILLIAN. Yes, for his sins. My parents want to meet him.

WESTON. I'd like to be a fly on the wall at that little powwow.

Everyone ignores him.

CLINTY. You'll love it, Rick, it's charming. Take some good walking shoes – Take him up on the downs, Gillian. Get some good clean air into his lungs.

There is a knock at the door.

WESTON. Enter!

SEALES *come in and stands by the door.*

Speak!

SEALES. Excuse me, sir, but Miss Dare and Miss Page were wondering if they could have the netball.

RICK. Yes, of course, Seales.

RICK *goes over to the cupboard and pulls out the ball and throws it over to* SEALES.

There you go.

SEALES *catches it and leaves.*

SEALES. Thanks, sir.

WESTON. Miss Dare? Miss Page? Good lord, Braithwaite, I hope you don't expect us all to address them like that? There's no Brownie points in it, you know?

RICK. What you do in your classroom is not my concern, Weston. But if you come into mine, I expect you to behave as courteously as the young men and women of my class will be to you.

CLINTY. It must be rubbing off on the other kids. Some of mine are calling the girls miss.

WESTON. Damned creepy if you ask me. I won't have it. Good God, you've got to know where you stand with 'em.

RICK. I believe basic manners in the classroom go a long way to making our job a lot easier. Mutual respect is important for the learning process.

WESTON. God, you're beginning to sound like the old man.

RICK. I'll take that as a compliment.

WESTON. Look, Braithwaite, I don't know how they went about it where you're from. Probably taught you too bloody much for your own good. But here, I say stick it on the blackboard and if they don't get it – tough. We're not here to turn out academics. Not in this school anyway.

RICK. Why not? Where 'I came from', Weston, we had half the facilities that you have here. Barely two rooms in the whole school. But what we did have were dedicated teachers who wanted the best for us. Irrespective of colour or class.

The school bell goes.

WESTON. Thank God, saved by the bell – or not in my case. I've got your lot for PE.

The others head out of the door as MR FLORIAN *comes in.* GILLIAN *gives* RICK *a rub on the back as she leaves. This noticed by* MR FLORIAN.

MR FLORIAN. Do I sense romance in the air, Braithwaite?

RICK *smiles.*

I'm so pleased. You make a lovely couple.

RICK. You think so?

MR FLORIAN. You should think of settling down. Starting a family. Time to put the war behind you.

RICK *starts to laugh. He pours himself some tea.*

Thought any more about what you're going to do about this place?

RICK. No, not really.

MR FLORIAN. The end of the year will be here before you know it.

RICK. It's gone so quickly. I've barely touched on what I was hoping to do.

MR FLORIAN. You're really getting involved with these children, aren't you?

RICK. I suppose we all are, one way or another.

MR FLORIAN. You're more involved than most.

RICK. I think Gillian's pretty serious.

MR FLORIAN. I think she's just passing time. She doesn't know it yet. That may make me sound rather chauvinistic but I assure you I'm not. Just my experience of teachers. I like Gillian, but I've seen teachers come and go. Not you, you've got a vocation.

RICK. My being here is just an accident. I'm not doing what I'm supposed to be doing.

MR FLORIAN. Aren't you?

RICK (*unsure*). No...

MR FLORIAN. You're a communicator, Rick, and communicators are few and far between. Every child remembers one teacher. No matter what their school experiences may be, there's always one that stands out from the rest. The one they'll remember for the rest of their lives. And whether you like it or not, you're going to be one of them.

RICK. I'm flattered.

MR FLORIAN. I don't flatter. It's a wonderful gift and sad for it not to be used with children. Especially children like ours, who, I think, need it more than most.

There is furious knocking at the door.

Come in.

The door opens and SEALES *stands there looking excited.*

SEALES. Sir, you've got to come quickly, Denham said he's going to kill Mr Weston. He's gonna smack his brains in with a bit of the vaulting horse!

RICK *heads quickly for the door.*

Scene Eight

The classroom.

DENHAM *and the other* BOYS *troop into the classroom still in their gym clothes.* RICK *follows them in. He is carrying the leg of the vaulting horse. The* BOYS *sit at their desks.*

RICK. Now, will somebody please explain to me what happened in the gym?

DENHAM. It was Weston's fault.

RICK. Mr Weston.

DENHAM. He knows Archie can't do the vault. He never does the vault.

EDWARDS. He made him do it, sir.

SEALES. Archie didn't want to, sir. Mr Weston just kept on at him, sir.

DENHAM. Kept saying, 'Come on, boy!' 'Jump, boy!' 'What's wrong with you!'

SEALES. He wouldn't leave off on him, sir. Just kept shouting and shouting at him.

SEALES. It wasn't right what he was doing, sir. Teachers shouldn't behave like that, sir. You know that, sir... Archie... He was crying, sir. You can't do that to someone...

ARCHIE. He just ran at the vault, sir.

SEALES. He didn't stand a chance. He just went flying. Denham just got angry, sir.

RICK. There is no excuse for your shocking conduct in the gym.

They all look shocked.

DENHAM. It was him that started it!

RICK. Mr Weston was the master in charge. Anything that happened in the gym was his responsibility.

DENHAM. But Archie told him he couldn't do it and he made him, sir.

RICK. I'm not concerned with Mr Weston's conduct, but with yours.

DENHAM. I thought Archie had really hurt himself. He was screaming on the floor.

RICK. So you rushed in like a hoodlum with your club to smash and kill, is that it? Suppose this was a knife or a gun, what then?

SEALES. Denham was narked, sir. We all were, seeing Archie on the floor like that, crying.

RICK. You're missing the point. Very soon you'll be at work and a lot of things will happen which will annoy you. Are you going to resort to knifes or clubs every time you get upset or are angered?

ARCHIE *comes back in followed by the* GIRLS, *obviously excited by the news.*

Come in. All of you, sit down. How are you feeling now, Archie?

ARCHIE. Better, sir.

RICK. Good lad. Sit yourself down.

ARCHIE. It wasn't Denham's fault, sir.

MONICA PAGE. Course it weren't.

ARCHIE. Mr Weston's always picking on me, sir. He knows I can never get over the vault.

RICK. Denham, you were discourteous to Mr Weston, and I believe you owe him an apology.

This causes consternation amongst the class.

DENHAM (*angry*). Why should I apologise? It was Weston that was in the wrong. You know he was in the wrong – I could see it in your face what you thought.

DENHAM *stands up angrily.*

What's wrong is wrong. That's what you say, isn't it? Or do your rules only apply if you're a teacher?

The whole class look at RICK.

RICK. That was a fair question. Although you will agree it was put a little, shall we say, indelicately?

RICK *smiles and so too does* DENHAM.

Are you truly pleased in the way you behaved with Mr Weston?

DENHAM. No, sir. But I couldn't help it, sir.

RICK. That may be so, Denham. But you agree your actions were wrong.

MONICA PAGE. Then what about Mr Weston apologising, to Archie?

PAMELA DARE. Yeah, what about him, sir?

There is a general consensus from the KIDS.

RICK. My concern is how your actions will be perceived.

SEALES. It's easy for you to talk, sir. Nobody tries to push you around.

RICK *gets up and walks over to where* SEALES *is sat.*

RICK. I've been pushed around, Seales, I've been pushed until I began to hate people so much that I wanted to hurt them, really hurt them. I think you all know what I'm talking about.

He looks at the class.

I know how it feels to hate. But the one thing I learned is to try always to be bigger than the people who hurt me.

RICK *realises the class has gone quiet and are listening to him. He walks to the front of the class.*

The point is, Denham, is whether you are really growing up and learning to stand on your own feet. In this instance, you lost your temper and behaved in an inappropriate manner to your teacher. Do you think you're man enough to accept you were wrong and go and apologise to him?

Beat.

Everyone looks at DENHAM.

DENHAM. Yes, sir.

Beat.

RICK. It's always difficult to apologise, especially to someone you feel justified in disliking. Remember you're not doing it for Mr Weston's sake, but your own.

DENHAM *stands up.*

DENHAM. Is he in the staffroom, sir?

SEALES *stands up too.*

SEALES. Sir, I think if Denham's big enough to apologise, I am too.

The other BOYS *stand up as well.*

RICK. Very well, gentlemen. You'll find Mr Weston in the staffroom.

The BOYS *all troop out behind* DENHAM.

RICK *sits looking at the* GIRLS *and* ARCHIE. *We can see the* BOYS *walk to the staffroom. Knock and go in.*

MONICA PAGE. I'm not saying anything me, sir. No, sir.

RICK. Good.

Beat.

MONICA PAGE. Nothing.

RICK. I'm glad.

MONICA PAGE. But... from what I gathered happened down there, there were – what's it me dad's lawyer said... Extenin...

RICK. Extenuating circumstances?

MONICA PAGE. That's it, sir. Extenuating circumstances in this case.

RICK. Yes, Miss Page. You're right, there were.

MONICA *is quite pleased with herself.*

MONICA PAGE. I could be a brief, me.

RICK. There's absolutely no reason why you couldn't take up the law, Miss Page. If you worked hard.

MONICA PAGE. I'd be dead good at that me, an' all. Hang 'im, hang 'im and hang 'im, an' all! No messin' about with me.

The GIRLS *start laughing, as the* BOYS *come back. This time followed by* WESTON.

WESTON. Mr Braithwaite, I wondered if I may address your class.

RICK *nods agreement and* WESTON *comes over and stands by the desk. The other* BOYS *all sit down.*

These boys have just apologised for the incident in the gym. I just wanted all of you to know that I too am sorry. As your teacher you were my responsibility and anything that happens is down to me and me alone. I think one way or another we were all a bit silly, but the sooner we forget about the whole incident the better.

He looks over at ARCHIE.

How are you feeling, Archie?

ARCHIE. Much better, sir.

WESTON. Good, good.

He nods to RICK *and heads out of the class.*

Beat.

MONICA PAGE. I'm sorry, sir, but... bleedin' 'ell!

They all start laughing. RICK *tries to hide the grin crossing his face.*

MR FLORIAN *appears at the door. He call* RICK *outside.* RICK *leaves and returns moments later. He looks shocked. He looks over at* SEALES.

RICK. Seales, why don't you get your things together. Mr Florian is outside. He wants a word with you. You're needed at home.

SEALES *stands up.*

SEALES. What is it, sir?

RICK. Maybe you should go along and see Mr Florian.

SEALES. It's me mum, innit, sir?

RICK *doesn't know what to say.*

Is she dead?

RICK. I'm sorry, Seales...

SEALES *suddenly starts to cry. It's a howl of pain. The other* KIDS *look on visibly shocked. A couple of the* GIRLS *start to cry as well.* RICK *goes over to* SEALES *and stands by his desk. He reaches out and puts his hand on his back.* SEALES *suddenly throws his arms around* RICK*'s waist.*

Scene Nine

The staffroom.

We hear the sound of rain. RICK *stands looking out of the window.*

CLINTY *comes in.*

CLINTY. You're in early?

RICK. So are you.

CLINTY. Early bird and all that.

RICK. Do you want some tea?

She nods. He pours her a cup.

CLINTY. Hey, how did your weekend with the prospective in-laws go? Did he take you out shooting? He's a very good shot, I seem to remember –

RICK. We didn't get that far.

CLINTY. Oh?

RICK *says nothing but just looks at her.*

That good, eh? Is it something you want to talk about?

RICK. I decided to cut the weekend short by about… Oh, the weekend.

CLINTY. Oh, Rick, what happened?

RICK. Let's just say Gillian's father decided it best to lay his cards on the table from the off, and leave it at that.

CLINTY. I'm sorry to hear about Seales' mother. Poor little blighter.

RICK. Mmmm, I felt so useless… I've spent so much time trying to get close to them, then something like this happens and I'm… What could I do…

CLINTY. You were there for him. That's all that matters. That's what's important.

RICK. What's going to happen to him now, he's the eldest of six, for God's sake? His father's just lost his job… I'm not cut out for this. The old man, thinks I have some kind of aptitude for teaching.

CLINTY. And he's right.

RICK. You think?

CLINTY. I know. You care about these kids. Really care. That's why you're worried about Seales. I'm not saying we don't, but most of us see four o'clock come round with a sense of relief. Not you. It bothers you what comes afterwards for these kids.

RICK. But I… I don't know if I want this… I didn't think for a minute it was going to be like this. I've applied for some electronics jobs.

CLINTY. Well, I for one would be sorry to see you go.

The door opens and GILLIAN *comes in.* CLINTY *stands and heads for the door.*

Morning, Gillian, I'm off to set up my stall. We're making bread-and-butter pudding today. Should be quite a ghastly experience. I'll save you a bit.

She heads out.

GILLIAN. I thought you were going to ring me when you got back?

RICK. Sorry, it seemed every telephone box I tried was out of order.

GILLIAN. I spoke to my father. He told me everything he'd said to you.

RICK. Did he?

GILLIAN. I can't tell you how angry I am with him.

RICK. Not angry enough to come back to London with me?

GILLIAN. How could I leave it like that? Will I still see you tonight? I've booked a table?

RICK. Yes.

He leaves.

Scene Ten

RICK *is looking for papers on his desk.*

MONICA PAGE. Please, sir.

RICK. Yes, Miss Page.

MONICA PAGE. Seales' mum, sir. She's being buried
tomorrow morning, sir.

RICK. Is she?

MONICA PAGE. We were wondering, sir. If we could have a
whip-round to buy a wreath.

RICK. I think that would be a wonderful gesture, Miss Page. I
think Seales would be very moved and grateful. May I be
allowed to contribute as well?

MONICA PAGE. Course you can, sir. Come on, you lot, get
your money out.

The other KIDS *start to hand* MONICA PAGE *their
contributions.* RICK *hands her his.*

PAMELA DARE. My auntie's got a flower stall, sir. She said
she'll do us up something lovely. Not cheap mind.

RICK. That's very kind of her.

PAMELA DARE. Mrs Seales used to do her washing for her,
see.

DENHAM. She did ours and all, sir. She worked at the
washhouse for years. Everyone knew her.

RICK. I'm sure the family will be very touched. Who will take
the wreath round to the house?

MONICA PAGE *stops what she's doing and they all look
at* RICK.

MONICA PAGE. The flowers, sir? Take the flowers?

RICK. Yes, who'll take them to the house?

MONICA PAGE (*apologetically*). We can't take them, sir.

RICK. What do you mean, Miss Page? Why can't you take them?

MONICA PAGE *looks about the class for help in explaining.*

MONICA PAGE. It's what people would say if they saw us going into a coloured person's house. You know… one of us girls, sir.

RICK. What they would say?

Suddenly the penny drops. RICK is struck dumb. He can't bring himself to speak. He looks at them. He's appalled, embarrassed and disappointed. He sits down in his chair. There is a pause of forty seconds, as he continues to look at them. He is unable to say anything. He looks out towards the window. The KIDS look at each other and at RICK but say nothing.

MONICA PAGE. Sir, I don't think you understood. We've got nothing against Seales. We like him. Honest we do, but if one of us girls was seen going to his house, into a coloured's… you can't imagine the things people would say… We'd be accused of all sorts.

RICK. Thank you for making that so clear, Miss Page. Does the same thing apply to the boys as well? Would it affect your honour in any way?

The BOYS can't bring themselves to look at RICK.

Very well –

PAMELA DARE stands up.

PAMELA DARE. I'll take them, sir.

RICK. Aren't you afraid of what might be said of you, Miss Dare?

PAMELA DARE. No, sir, gossips don't worry me. Besides I've know Larry – Seales, since we were in the infants together.

RICK. Thank you, Miss Dare. I'll see you there tomorrow.

The bell rings.

You'd better go.

The KIDS head off looking embarrassed and subdued. MR FLORIAN comes in as they go out.

MR FLORIAN. They're usually full of beans coming out of here? What on earth's happened?

RICK. My kids won't deliver a funeral wreath to the Seales' house, because of what people might think of them. Going into a coloured person's home.

MR FLORIAN. Oh, my dear fellow –

RICK. It's a wreath, for God's sake! The boy's mother's dead! Can there be no compassion even in death?

MR FLORIAN. This bears no reflection on you, Rick.

RICK. Doesn't it? What in God's name have I been doing all these months then? Have I been wasting my time? Have I taught them nothing... I thought they liked me – I thought they'd begun to respect me, but this?

MR FLORIAN. They do respect you. The very fact that they stood there and told you, shows they don't agree with it. And that's down to you and the relationship you have with them. They're as appalled as you are.

RICK. Are they?

MR FLORIAN. Yes. But they have to live here and unfortunately that is how many people think. You can't stamp out prejudice overnight. But you've got a classroom full of young people that you're sending out into the world. They've learned from you. You've taught them to think differently. That's how we beat the bigotry, class by class. Year after year.

Scene Eleven

Street.

RICK *and* GILLIAN *walk onto the stage.*

GILLIAN. I'm sorry, we should never have gone there.

RICK. We had to eat somewhere.

Beat.

GILLIAN. Why didn't you say something, Rick? Why did you just sit there and take it?

RICK. I suppose you're referring to the waiter?

GILLIAN (*angry*). Who else would I be referring to?

She brings her voice back down.

RICK. What was I supposed to do, hit him? Did you want a scene in that place?

GILLIAN. Yes, I wanted a scene. I wanted the biggest scene you could have come up with!

RICK. What good would that have done?

GILLIAN. I don't know and I don't care. But I wanted you to do something. You should have hit him. Beat him hard.

RICK. It wouldn't help, it never does.

GILLIAN. Why not? Just who do you think you are, Jesus Christ? You just sat there all good and patient. Were you afraid? Is that it? Were you afraid of that damned little waiter, that wretched little peasant of a waiter?

RICK. Beating people up doesn't solve anything.

GILLIAN. Doesn't it? Well, what does?

RICK. I thought you knew me a little better than that, Gillian.

GILLIAN. You've been taking it and taking it, don't you think it's time you showed a bit of spirit?

RICK. What is it, Gillian?

GILLIAN. Why is it always someone else fighting your fight? Everyone stands up for you against Weston –

RICK. I don't need them to.

GILLIAN. And me, Rick, was I meant to stand up for you tonight? Or was I suppose to sit and watch that disgusting, bigoted little man humiliate you because of your colour? You should have given him a good slap across the face.

She makes to move off. RICK *grabs her arm and turns her.*

RICK. And is that what I should have done to your father?

GILLIAN. Let go of me.

RICK. No, you're going to listen. You think it's perfectly acceptable to beat up a waiter because of his obvious racism. But when it comes to a nice middle-class gentleman, like your father, you expect me to sit there and take it?

GILLIAN. That's not what I'm saying.

RICK. At least the waiter was honest. He didn't hide his disgust at my colour with phony sugar-coated platitudes of sympathy.

He mimics GILLIAN's *middle-class father.*

'You're a very nice chap, Rick, charming intelligent – but you're a Negro.' 'Have you considered your children, Rick? What will happen to them? They won't belong anywhere, Rick.' Well pardon me, Mr Blanchard, for lumbering you with a couple of piccaninnies to play with on the village green!

GILLIAN. That's not what he –

RICK. That's exactly what he meant! Don't you think I wanted to smash his face in too? Don't you think I wanted to wring his scrawny little neck!

GILLIAN. Stop it, Rick, you're making it all sound so ugly!

RICK. It is ugly, Gillian, and it'll get uglier!

GILLIAN. I don't want to hear it!

RICK. The looks of disgust, the snide remarks, people spitting at you in the street. This is what a relationship with me, means! Your family turns their back on you. Friends stop calling.

GILLIAN. No –

RICK. Yes. All that and more! Much more!

They both calm down.

GILLIAN. I never thought…

RICK (*incredulous*). Didn't you know that such things happened?

GILLIAN. I'd heard and read about it, but… My parents were… It's as if I suddenly didn't know who they were. I never imagined it happening to me.

RICK. It needn't happen again.

GILLIAN. What do you mean? Is that what you want, Rick?

RICK. No. Of course it isn't. But I have to be sure that you do.

GILLIAN. I think I'm in love with you. But I'm afraid now. Everything seemed alright before, now it's all so frightening. I just don't understand how you take it so calmly. Don't you mind?

RICK. I do mind. But I've learnt how to mind and still live.

GILLIAN. I don't know if I'm going to be strong enough.

RICK. No, I don't know if you are either.

She runs off, leaving RICK *alone.*

Scene Twelve

The street.

RICK *stands alone. He is joined by* MR FLORIAN, *who walks on carrying a funeral wreath.*

MR FLORIAN. Thought you might need some company.

RICK. Thank you, sir.

> PAMELA DARE *enters carrying the wreath.*

Hello, Miss Dare. It's good to see you here.

> *Suddenly all the other* KIDS *walk onto the stage and join them.* RICK *says nothing but just looks at them proudly.*

DENHAM. It's traditional to walk behind the hearse for a few streets, sir.

RICK. Thank you, Mr Denham.

MONICA PAGE. Here it comes now, sir.

PAMELA DARE. We just fall in behind it, sir.

MONICA PAGE. There's Seales. He's looking at us.

> *A few of the* KIDS *give little embarrassed waves.*

DENHAM. Come on, sir.

> MR FLORIAN *smiles at* RICK.

MR FLORIAN. Class by class, year after year.

> *They all start to walk slowly off the stage.*

Scene Thirteen

The staffroom.

Late afternoon. The room is decorated with paper lanterns.
WESTON *is sat snoozing in his chair.* RICK *is standing by the*
pigeonholes cleaning his out, dropping the rubbish into a
waste-paper basket he holds. We can hear the excited cries of
the KIDS *in the playground.* CLINTY *is sat, looking exhausted.*

CLINTY. Well at least that's over for another year.

RICK. You must be exhausted, Clinty. I've never seen such a
collection of cakes.

WESTON. You must be teaching them something, old girl,
because they didn't taste half bad either.

CLINTY. End of term. Everything comes together as if by magic.

WESTON. What about you, Braithwaite, how was it for you?

RICK. I must admit. I really quite enjoyed it.

RICK *pulls out a letter. He looks at the address. He puts*
down the waste basket and opens the letter. RICK *reads*
the letter.

My God!

CLINTY. What is it?

RICK. My birthday has come early this year. I've been offered
a job with an electronics company. In Birmingham.

CLINTY. But Rick, that's wonderful! Well done. You know my
thoughts on the matter, but I'm very pleased for you.

RICK. I don't believe it.

WESTON. You mean you're buggering off?

RICK. It would seem that way.

WESTON. But you can't!

Everybody looks at WESTON, *surprised.*

You make those delinquents almost agreeable to teach, for
God's sake. What are we going to do with the next lot if
you're not here?

CLINTY. You hardly make anyone welcome, Weston.

WESTON. Oh, don't mind me. That's just my way. I'm rude and bigoted to everyone. Even my parents disliked me. They said so often. You can't possibly want to go to Birmingham.

RICK. Why?

WESTON. Well, well there's that extraordinarily awful accent for starters.

GILLIAN comes in.

CLINTY. Guess what, Rick's got a new job.

GILLIAN. Really?

She looks at RICK.

RICK. Yes.

GILLIAN. That's wonderful, Rick. I'm really very pleased for you.

RICK. Thank you, Gillian.

GILLIAN. Good luck.

She picks up her bag and heads out.

Have a lovely summer, all of you.

CLINTY. Aren't you stopping for the seniors' dance?

GILLIAN. No, I can't. Bye, bye...

She glances at RICK as she leaves.

WESTON. You know, it's a bit rum if you ask me. Abandoning ship like this mid-ocean.

CLINTY. We're hardly the *Titanic*, Weston.

WESTON. I'm surprised at you, Rick. Waste of a good teacher.

CLINTY and RICK look surprised. WESTON has called RICK by his first name. They find it amusing but cover their smiles.

RICK. I'm sorry you feel that way, erm...

RICK *looks at* WESTON *questioningly. All eyes are on* WESTON.

WESTON.…Humphrey…

RICK. Well, Humphrey, I shall miss you too.

There is a knock at the door.

WESTON. Enter!

PAMELA DARE c*omes into the room. She is dressed up and looks wonderful.*

Yes, Miss Dare. What can we do for you this fine day?

PAMELA DARE. I've brought some invitations for our dance, sir. Do you think I could hand them out?

WESTON. But of course.

PAMELA DARE *comes in and starts to hand out the invitations.*

RICK. You're looking lovely today, Miss Dare.

PAMELA DARE. Thank you, sir.

She hands them out. She goes over to WESTON *and gives one to him.*

WESTON. Me?

PAMELA DARE. Yes, sir…

WESTON. You're inviting me?

PAMELA DARE. If you want to come, sir.

WESTON. Erm, I'd be delighted…

RICK *goes over to the door and opens it for her. Just as he's closing it –*

PAMELA DARE. Oh, sir.

RICK. Yes, Miss Dare?

PAMELA DARE. Will you have a dance with me tonight?

RICK. Of course, Miss Dare. I'd be honoured. But no jiving –
I'm getting too old for that.

She smiles.

PAMELA DARE. Okay, sir, I'll bring in a special record for
you. Promise?

RICK. Yes, Miss Dare. I promise.

PAMELA DARE. And, sir.

RICK. Yes?

PAMELA DARE. Will you call me Pamela, just for this
evening?

RICK. Of course, Pamela.

PAMELA DARE *smiles widely.*

PAMELA DARE. Thank you.

She walks off.

CLINTY. You've just given that young girl the best leaving
present ever!

WESTON. I've been invited to the party.

They look at WESTON *and start laughing.*

*We hear Bill More singing 'We're Going to Rock' as the
lights fade.*

Scene Fourteen

The gym.

The gymnasium has been decorated for the party. The KIDS *are all dressed up and dancing.* MR FLORIAN *is having a go as only old people dancing to modern music can, to the delight of the* KIDS. WESTON *is acting as DJ. He yanks off the record to a chorus of groans.*

WESTON. Erm, the next record I am about to play for you is called 'It Takes a Long Tall Brown-skin Gal' by the Four Blues.

He pops on the record and everyone starts to dance again.

CLINTY. I think Humphrey's found a new calling.

RICK. I think you may be right.

CLINTY. Listen, Rick, tell me if I'm sticking my big nose in but I spoke to Gillian. She told me everything that happened. You know she's not coming back next term?

RICK. You're sticking your big nose in.

CLINTY. Right.

RICK. Look, Clinty, what happened, happened for the best. It could have been a lot worse further along down the line.

MR FLORIAN *comes over, wiping his brow.*

MR FLORIAN. I somehow manage to impress them with my terpsichorean knowledge every year.

CLINTY. You certainly do, Headmaster!

MR FLORIAN. The trick is to keep up with them. Every year without fail, I nip down to my local ballroom and learn the latest steps.

RICK. You're very good, sir.

MR FLORIAN. And you both know how to flatter an old man.

They laugh.

Clinty tells me you're going to be leaving us.

RICK. I've been offered a position, sir.

MR FLORIAN. It's what you wanted, I believe?

RICK. Yes, sir. Very much so.

MR FLORIAN. Well, you deserve it, Braithwaite. But I'll hate to lose you.

PAMELA DARE comes over to them.

WESTON changes the record again with a scratch.

WESTON. The next dance is a ladies' excuse-me foxtrot. 'In the Still of the Night'. By Cole Porter.

RICK. I think this is our dance, Pamela.

PAMELA DARE. I think it is, sir.

They dance elegantly around the floor. Other dancers stop to watch. PAMELA DARE is in seventh heaven as she allows RICK to glide her about the floor. As the music stops everyone claps.

RICK. Thank you, Pamela.

PAMELA DARE. Thank you, sir.

DENHAM starts to clap his hands to gain attention.

DENHAM. Hello, could I have your attention, please. Mr Weston, sir. The music.

WESTON turns off the music.

Thank you. Erm, I'd like to say a few words on behalf of the senior year.

The others gather around DENHAM. DENHAM takes out a prepared speech.

I know you others have taught us as well. But this is for sir –

MONICA PAGE. Mr Braithwaite, dummy.

The others giggle.

RICK. Sir will do, Denham.

DENHAM. We just wanted to say how grateful we are for all you've done for us in the short time you've been our teacher. We know it hasn't been a bed of roses for you, what with one thing and another. And we could have given you an easier time at first. But if we had you wouldn't have loved us as much as you do now!

They all laugh.

We think we're much better people for having had you as our teacher. And we liked the way you treated us as adults and the way you spoke and did things... We... we...

He looks up at RICK *and at the rest of the class. He screws up the speech.*

We just wanted to say, thank you, sir... For me... I don't know what you did, sir... and it might well sound stupid to anyone else... but you made me feel like I've been somewhere, you know? These last months and that. Somewhere I'd like to go back to one day... I think if I have kids – if any of us have kids – we'd like them to be taught by a man like you, sir. Because I think they'd be safe in your hands.

DENHAM *looks at* SEALES. SEALES *walks over to* RICK *and hands him a present wrapped in ribbon.* RICK *takes it.*

RICK. Thank you, Seales.

He opens the card.

MONICA PAGE. Read it out, sir.

RICK. 'To sir with love...'

He doesn't get any further. He knows if he attempts to say another thing he'll end up in pieces. The KIDS *sense it and start clapping. Everyone else joins in.* RICK *turns and heads for the classroom.* WESTON *starts to sing 'For He's a Jolly Good Fellow'.*

WESTON.
     'For he's a jolly good fellow!
     For he's a jolly good fellow!'

All the others join in the song.

ALL.

'For he's a jolly good fellow.
And so say all of us.
And so say all of us.
And so say all of us.'

The light fades in the gym.

Lights up in the classroom.

RICK *stands by his desk listening to the singing. He opens the present. It's a silver frame. He takes out the letter from his inside pocket.*

'For he's a jolly good fellow!
For he's a jolly good fellow!
For he's a jolly good fellow.
And so say all of us.
And so say all of us.
And so say all of us.'

He tears it up as the lights begin to fade.

The End.